WACO-McLENNAN COUN
1717 AUSTIN A\
WACO TX 767(

Designing Programmes

four essays and an introduction	by Karl Gerstner
with an introduction to the introduction	by Paul Gredinger
first published	by Arthur Niggli Ltd., Teufen AR (Switzerland), 1964
original blocks	by Neue Chemiegraphie AG Zurich
originally printed	by Brin + Tanner AG Basle
originally bound	by Max Grollimund Basle
English version	by D. Q. Stephenson

Facsimile edition 2019	edited by Lars Müller
© 2019 Lars Müller Publishers and Estate of Karl Gerstner	www.lars-mueller-publishers.com
Printed in Germany	ISBN 978-3-03778-578-2

Lars Müller Publishers

Paul Gredinger:

Pro-Programmatic

Do you know what the title of the book means? The title of the book can be explained by reference to the book title. A programme can be designed for naming the book. For this, one must know what the book is about. The subject, at any rate, is: creative arrangement. But that is too general. As the author sees it, there are two separate aspects to creative arrangement: the design, to design, the designer, etc. and the programme, to programme, programmatic, etc. Well then, Design and Programme? No. The "and" is too weak. The two ideas are more closely linked than that. Programme Design? Design Programme? No. Both are dependent on each other. Which on which? Each on each. Design of the Programme? Programme of the Design? No. To be sure, the meaning of both is clear. But what is essential lies in between. It lies in the designation of the two ideas. The principal question, then, is the connection between the two words. It can be expressed through any kind of linguistic link. For the reciprocal action of programme and design should be as complete as possible. The solution: to enumerate all the possible ways in which these concepts can be connected. And to consider all these variants as a book title. The best solution would be to list them all together on the cover: Design of Programmes, Programme for Design. Design = Programme. Programming. Designing. Programming Designs. Designing Programmes. And so forth. The book would have to feature a whole list of titles. Since that is not possible, the title reads as it is now. But means an entire programme.

The title can be explained in different terms. Designing programmes can also mean: inventing rules of arrangement. Taking a chemical reaction as a parallel, the designer must try to find a group of new combinations by reference to a kind of formula. The formula is paramount. The formula creates the form. Creates a group of forms. Thus, for instance, there is a formula in poetry corresponding to this conception. The traditional structure of language is dissolved. No grammar. No syntax. The elements are single words. They stand loose in the line with all their valencies free. The rule of the game is permutation. The poems arising are called constellations. Constellations are a poetic programme. There is an example in this book.

Another example of a programme (and as usual the programme comprises certain elements and certain rules for combining them): four pictorial signs each having nine values are printed on cards: Swiss jass cards. The rules for their combination are the rules of jass. The rule of the game = programme. And, considered in these terms, every other game is nothing more than the carrying out of a programme.

More self-evident still, and hence all the less consciously present in one's mind: the formula of the recipe. First the elements are enumerated: take . . . potatoes, milk, water, salt, and butter. Then the preparation: peeling, cutting up, boiling, straining, stirring . . . Result: creamed potatoes. The recipe is the programme. Simple enough. But interpreting many of these programmes is more difficult. And when it comes to designing them, then the difficulties really begin. That is why it is called an art. The culinary art. And then there is still the whole menu to cook: one programme superimposed on another. The full score is a cookery book.

And then a surprisingly obvious example is provided by another of the housewife's occupations: making something linear into something two-dimensional or even something with a complicated spatial form. And to make it by simple means. What is topologically complicated is simply called: knitting. Programme: in – round – through – off. Result: knitting. Another variant of the programme produces purling. More complicated rules produce more complicated patterns. The programme is contained in any instructions for a knitting pattern. In machine knitting the programme is a punched tape. Example: Jacquard pattern.

Example of a programme that has become a picture: the ornament. For instance: a scissor-cut. Or: kaleidoscope. Two pictures harking back to childhood? Yet there is more behind them than meets the eye. There is a whole world behind them. The simplest elements (form) fitted together in the simplest way (repetition, symmetry) give expression to the spirit of an entire culture. China, South America, Asia Minor, Africa, Greece, Rome. And the geometrical art of today?

Closest to the typical idea of a structural programme come structures in electronic music. Here the structural unity of the mental vision is realized by projection into the musical experience. The elements of the composition are sound units (impulses). Composing with these units consists in regulating a single parameter: time. And the music is a structure of programmed impulses. Structure in the sense of the organization of growth.

Another example of a programme as a formulated predetermination is provided by any musical score. Particular interest attaches to written instructions which make disorder (the most random arrangement) and not order their governing principle. The following example is explained in the book. A composer lets random features of the surface of the paper determine frequency, duration, timbre, volume and entry. The sounds are not predetermined as usual. All the same, the score is a score, a designed programme: that and that are the elements. And I can do that with them. Result: a whole series of solutions. It is not important that the result should be this or that; what is important is that the form should and must take its shape in obedience to an order or formula. It is in the design of the formula (image: a tulip bulb) and not in the design of the form (image: tulip) that the creative pleasure resides. And thus the aim of the creative work.

Without programme

I am very pleased that this book has been brought to fruition and I should like to thank all those who have had a share in it. If I were to make up a programme of what and more particularly who had been indispensable in producing this small book, I should finish up with an astonishingly long list. I should first have to mention my secretary, Béatrice Preiswerk, who has had the job of converting my MSS with loving care into legible typescripts. I should have to go farther, and by way of my friend Hans Tanner, who has become the owner of a printing works since my first book, his foreman, the machine compositor, the caster, the jobbing compositor, the proof puller and the proof reader, I should come by devious routes to you the reader. And in every case – and more particularly yours – I should have cause to express thanks for the friendly interest shown. To be brief: the printing costs, which are high enough as they are, would be higher still. So, in the interests of both parties, we will not make a programme (There are cases, you see!)

Kindly allow me, however, to revert to certain people to whom I feel under a particular and personal obligation. Paul Gredinger, partner in the Agency (and incidentally one of the first to compose electronic music, i. e. programmed music par excellence, and also the inventor of the concept of the serial) a versatile and stimulating personality who, among other things, introduced us to the morphological method, is particularly deserving of my thanks for the introductory introduction, which not only expresses what I mean but has also put some new ideas into my own mind. I should also like to thank Markus Kutter, my second partner, for letting me use his "Programme for Berio", which is published here for the first time. I am also pleased to acknowledge that I was glad of his literary help in formulating the title.

I should also like to thank my staff in the Gerstner, Gredinger and Kutter Advertising Agency for their collaboration, of which they may not be aware: all the work which is quoted as an example in the introduction and the first two essays and where the author is not explicitly mentioned has been produced by a team and is not my own work. At most my work was restricted to designing the programme (and not always that). Among the staff I should like to mention in particular the photographers (and especially the head of the photographic studio, Alexander von Steiger) who were called upon largely in connection with the last two essays and accomplished a difficult task well. It is a pleasure for me to thank Vera Spoerri for the pastework picture in the introduction and John Cage for his kind permission to print his Variations I. And finally I should like to thank Ida and Arthur Niggli for including my programmes in their publishing programme although the essays had already been published before, albeit in widely scattered places, namely:

"The Old Berthold Sans-Serif on a New Basis" in the *Druckspiegel*, No. 6, June 1963 at the invitation of Kurt Weidemann. The head of the Druckspiegelverlag in Stuttgart, K. Kohlhammer, kindly placed the blocks at my disposal.

"Integral Typography" as the leading article in the special number of the *Typographische Monatsblätter* of the same name, published by Rudolf Hostettler, Numbers 5/6 June/July 1959, Verlag Zollikofer St. Gal (supplemented by some new examples and a bibliography.)

"Making Pictures Today?" in the international magazine for art and literature *Spirale*, No. 8, September 1960, published by Spiral Press, Berne. The publisher Marcel Wyss also kindly permitted the blocks to be used here, for which grateful thanks are expressed (again supplemented with some illustrations).

"Structure and Movement" (appearing shortly) in a collection of writings by contemporary designers, which Gyorgy Kepes is bringing out under the title *"Vision and Values"* and which will be published by Georges Braziller Inc. New York. (Revised and expanded).

Karl Gerstner, Ascona, September 11, 1963

Designing Programmes

four essays and an introduction
by Karl Gerstner

The idea for this book came from Japan, from Naomi Asakura. He wrote that he was a designer and teacher in Fukushima-shi. He wanted (he said) to publish my first book – "Cold Art" – in Tokyo. He thought the analyses it contained of concrete pictures were of educational use and worth translating. The chapter that was of most personal interest to him was the last one entitled "Prospects of the Future". This chapter (he said) had been written in 1957. Thus the future was now behind us. What were the prospects now?

He wondered if I had written something more topical on the subject in the meantime. If topicality is to be measured in terms of dates, – well, there are these essays. A testament in advance? I should prefer the reader to interpret this collection with the same open mind as that with which they were conceived: as an interim balance, the result of experience which can be supplemented or rejected at will in each part.

This story really leads up to the point: as I wanted to see to the typography of the Far Eastern edition, Asakura sent me a selection of Japanese typefaces.

It was not easy for me to find criteria and make my choice. I do not understand what the signs mean and the feeling for design they embody is foreign to me. But the picture below fascinates me. One thing I did understand: the Japanese have evolved a programme from a typeface; they have achieved something which will still keep us busy for a long time to come. (The reader will understand this after reading the first essay "A new Basis for the Old Display Sans-Serif".

1

変形レンズで次の様になります。□
を使用すると此の様な感じです。□
を使用すると此の様な感じです。□
を使用すると此の様な感じです。□
を使用すると此の様な感じです。□
を使用すると此の様な感じです。□
を使用すると此の様な感じです。□
を使用すると此の様な感じです。□
を使用すると此の様な感じです。□
を使用すると此の様な感じです。□
を使用すると此の様な感じです。□

Programme from the Far Middle Ages

I pass the Cathedral every day on my way to work. The building contains some typical Gothic specialities. An example is provided by the pointed arches of the 15th century cloisters reproduced below: a perfect example of the joyful (and artful) way the Gothic designers went to work.

Joyful, because it gave them pleasure to create complicated patterns in profusion. Artful, because they tempered the complicacy to the beholder and concealed the profusion. That is: none of the 16 windows (one is missing in the picture) is identical with another; simply because somebody wanted to have fun (a whim, perhaps, of the head artisan?) Each window is a design in itself based on an exact programme of constants and variants.

The Programme:
The material and execution are prescribed; the dimensions, outlines, including the vertical tripartition up to the springing line of the arch.

There are 16 different ornamental patterns to be designed in the triangle of the arch and they must be related from the following points of view:

the profiles of the lines and the joining together of the bundles of lines are in principle all alike – the tracing of the lines must be adapted organically to the outline and also to the vertical tripartition – the lines meet either at right angles to each other (or to the periphery) or run into each other at 0 degrees – there must be no residual forms; that is, each line must form a self-contained pattern on two sides.

Programme as morphology

Unbounded surfaces

Example.
To give at least one instance of the astonishing richness and beauty of such geometrical patterns, Fig. 5 to 20 show forms which can be obtained in a latticework from a square consisting of $3^2 = 9$ part squares by drawing a straight line between any two nodes. The number of nodes here is 16, which happens to be the same as the number of connecting lines between them and therefore also the number of patterns of the first order. Each total square 3^2 is repeated four times in juxtaposition so as to show the connection thus established between the single patterns (Fig. 5).

In patterns 5 to 8 the "theme", i.e. the line being multiplied in conformity to a rule (here the fourfold reflection of the square is being used), lies either minus a side of a square or in an axis of reflection, so that there are only four repetitions at a time. They make the simpler, more familiar forms. The other patterns are developed from lines in another position, each of which yields eight repetitions. The forms thus arising are largely unknown.

Each of the 16 forms can be combined with every other one in a pattern of the second order. They can be easily drawn if first one pattern is introduced into the lattice-work and then the other is drawn over it.

If three are drawn over one another, a pattern of the third order is obtained, of which there are 560.

From: "Harmonie der Formen" by Wilhelm Ostwald. Verlag Unesma, Leipzig 1927

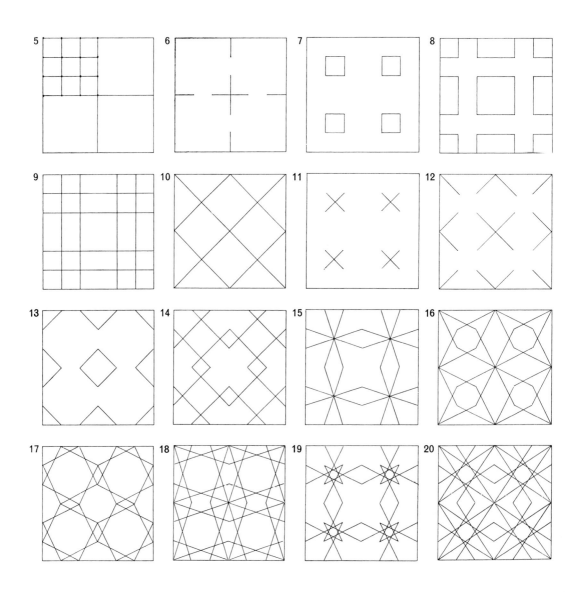

Programme as Logic

Instead of solutions for problems, programmes for solutions – the subtitle can also be understood in these terms: for no problem (so to speak) is there an absolute solution. Reason: the possibilities cannot be delimited absolutely. There is always a group of solutions, one of which is the best under certain conditions.

To describe the problem is part of the solution. This implies: not to make creative decisions as prompted by feeling but by intellectual criteria. The more exact and complete these criteria are, the more creative the work becomes. The creative process is to be reduced to an act of selection. Designing means: to pick out determining elements and combine them. Seen in these terms, designing calls for method. The most suitable I know is the one Fritz Zwicky has developed, although actually his is intended for scientists rather than designers. (*Die morphologische Forschung*, 1953, Kommissionsverlag, Winterthur) I have produced the diagram below in accordance with his instructions and, following his terminology, I have called it the morphological box of the typogram. It contains the criteria – the parameters on the left, the relative components on the right – following which marks and signs are to be designed from letters.

The criteria are rough. As the work proceeds, of course, they are to be refined as desired. The components are to be made into parameters and new components are to be specified, etc. Moreover, they are not only rough, they are also not self-contained. The component "something else" is the parcel in which the left-overs are packed if the parameter does not break down neatly. The designations are imprecise in some cases. There are many imperfections. But it is precisely in drawing up the scheme, in striving for perfection, that the work really lies. The work is not diminished; it is merely transferred to another plane.

The inadequacy of this box is my own and not inherent in the method. Even so: it contains thousands of solutions which – as could be shown by checking an example – are arrived at by the blind concatenation of components. It is a kind of designing automatic.

a Basis

1. Components	11. Word	12. Abbreviation	13. Word group	14. Combined	
2. Typeface	21. Sans-serif	22. Roman	23. German	24. Some other	25. Combined
3. Technique	31. Written	32. Drawn	33. Composed	34. Some other	35. Combined

b Colour

1. Shade	11. Light	12. Medium	13. Dark	14. Combined	
2. Value	21. Chromatic	22. Achromatic	23. Mixed	24. Combined	

c Appearance

1. Size	11. Small	12. Medium	13. Large	14. Combined	
2. Proportion	21. Narrow	22. Usual	23. Broad	24. Combined	
3. Boldness	31. Lean	32. Normal	33. Fat	34. Combined	
4. Inclination	41. Upright	42. Oblique	43. Combined		

d Expression

1. Reading direction	11. From left to right	12. From top to bottom	13. From bottom to top	14. Otherwise	15. Combined
2. Spacing	21. Narrow	22. Normal	23. Wide	24. Combined	
3. Form	31. Unmodified	32. Mutilated	33. Projected	34. Something else	35. Combined
4. Design	41. Unmodified	42. Something omitted	43. Something replaced	44. Something added	45. Combined

Solutions from the programme

(Not all the solutions were found with the aid of the morphological box. But all those found can be assigned to a place in it and analyzed.)

If all the components contained in the trademark *intermöbel* are added we obtain the following chain:

a 11. (word) – 21. (sans-serif) – 33. (composed)
b 14. (shades combined, viz. light and dark) – 12. (achromatic)
c 12. (size immaterial, therefore medium) – 22. (proportion usual) – 33. (fat) – 41. (roman)
d 11. (from left to right) – 22. (normal spacing) – 31. (form unmodified) – 43. (something replaced, viz. the face of the letter r by superimposition of the two parts of the word).

Not all the components are of equal importance; only two are actually decisive: b 14 + d 43.

The importance of "combined" is shown in example b 14: the components light-medium-dark are not very expressive in themselves because they do not represent an assessable value (apart from black always being dark). But if letters of varying degrees of darkness are combined (as here) the parameter of shade may be the point at which the solution crystallizes out.

Parameters as points of crystallization: I will illustrate all those in the section "Expression" by the following examples:

"Reading direction" determines the expression of the typograms *Krupp* and *National Zeitung*. In both instances the component d 15 (combined) forms the basis. In *Krupp* d 11 (from left to right) is combined with d 14 (otherwise, i. e. from right to left).
In the case of *National Zeitung* the components are d 12 and 13. Incidentally, the typogram for Bech Electronic Centre belongs here, see page 44.

"Spacing", once again combined in the component, is determining in *Braun Electric* and *Autokredit A.G.*

22

intermöbel

23

ᴚᴚ∩ꟼꟼ 1811
KRUPP 1961

24

25

B r a u n Electric International SA

26

AUTO K R E D I T

Again: Solutions from the programme

"Form" is relevant in *Abfälle, Globotyper, wievoll?*. In *Abfälle* the component d 32 (mutilated, here fragmented); in *Globotyper* d 33 (projected, here on a sphere), in *wievoll?* d 34 (something else, the form is neither unmodified, nor is it mutilated or projected, but "something else": partly silhouetted).

The idea of "design" means something more than is conveyed by "form". To take an example: in *Auto AG*, the dropping of the crossbar of the A's cannot be called a mutilation nor a form operation either. If the form is mutilated, the components are preserved. That is not the case in this instance. The form as such is Berthold sans-serif but "something is omitted". The reverse applies to the case of *FH* (Fédération Horlogère Suisse): here "something is added": namely, the Swiss cross within the letters. In the case of *Rheinbrücke* there is "something replaced": the part of the word "brücke" (bridge) by the sign.

The reader will have noticed that there is a criterion running right through the examples below: the relationship between form and content.

Basically, every typogram can be produced in two ways: firstly, through the word sense (to interpret the meaning) and secondly, through the word picture (to take the formal data as the point of departure). It would need a second, a semantic box, to bring this within a system. Its components can be found in the examples given here.

Say: the solution for *National Zeitung* is the perception of a formal rotation, *Krupp* is a literary interpretation (Look back to the past, look forward to the future). In *Autokredit* the word credit (payment over a long term) is represented. In *Globotyper* the typeface suggests the typewriter and the projection suggests the sphere (it was originally a name for the IBM spherical head typewriter). "*Abfälle*" and "*wievoll?*" symbolize the idea, etc.

27

28

globotyper

29

wievoll?

30

ΛUTO ΛG

31

32

RHEIN

Programme as Grid

Is the grid a programme? Let me put it more specifically: if the grid is considered as a proportional regulator, a system, it is a programme par excellence. Squared paper is a (arithmetic) grid, but not a programme. Unlike, say, the (geometric) module of Le Corbusier, which can, of course, be used as a grid but is primarily a programme. Albert Einstein said of the module: "It is a scale of proportions that makes the bad difficult and the good easy". That is a programmatic statement of what I take to be the aim of "Designing Programmes".

The typographic grid is a proportional regulator for composition, tables, pictures, etc. It is a formal programme to accommodate x unknown items. The difficulty is: to find the balance, the maximum of conformity to a rule with the maximum of freedom. Or: the maximum of constants with the greatest possible variability.

In our agency we have evolved the "mobile grid". An example is the arrangement below: the grid for the periodical *Capital*.

The basic unit is 10 points; the size of the basic typeface including the lead. The text and picture area are divided at the same time into one, two, three, four, five and six columns. There are 58 units along the whole width. This number is a logical one when there are always two units between the columns. That is: it divides in every case without a remainder: with two columns the 58 units are composed of 2 x 28 + 2 (space between columns); with 3 columns 3 x 18 + 2 x 2; with 4 columns 4 x 13 + 3 x 2; with 5 columns 5 x 10 + 4 x 2; with 6 columns 6 x 8 + 5 x 2 10-point units.

The grid looks complicated to anyone not knowing the key. For the initiate it is easy to use and (almost) inexhaustible as a programme.

33

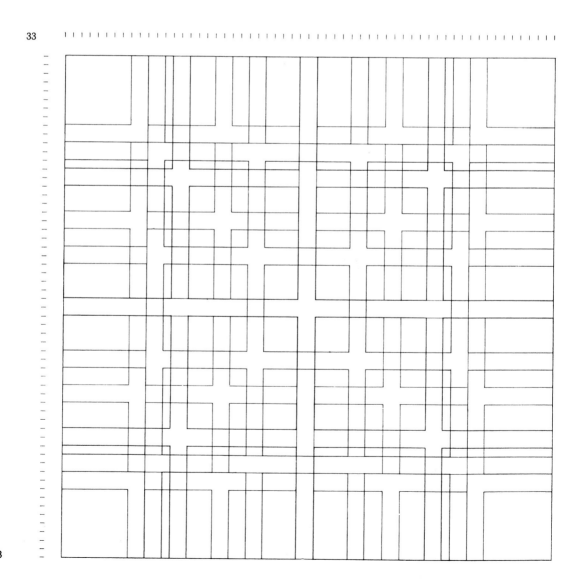

Again: Programme as Grid

The grid meant here is the screen of a printing block. A good example for understanding an essential factor.

Designing programmes means finding a generally valid principle of integrated arrangement. This applies not only to typography (a predestined application in any case) or – going farther afield – to the realm of geometry. It applies without any restriction to the realm of the visual. Without restriction because all the elements are programmable periodically, i. e. at will. There is no dimension, proportion, form; no colour, which cannot be constantly led over into another. All the elements occur in series, or better, in groups.

The same applies in the realm of the acoustic, in music. Language is different, because the elements have not been produced naturally but artificially. Even if programming in literature is subject to restricted laws, it is still quite possible, as is shown by Kutter's Programme for Berio.

The periodic demonstrated by the block screen: a light tone consists of small, black dots on a white surface; a dark tone is the reverse. Between them is the arithmetically exact grey tone: a checkerwork of black and white squares of equal size. Thus, from light to dark, the screen undergoes a transformation from circle to square to circle, in which process the form changes as steadily as the tone.

In the colour block there is the added fascination of the colour mixture: out of 4 colours (yellow-purple-cyan-black) all the colours can be produced periodically simply by manipulating the size of the half-tone screen dots.

What could have been more logical than to take the screen itself as a sign programme for a block-making factory? Fig. 34: the minimum form declared to be a form is integrated into a larger whole in the other three examples (advertisement subjects).

34
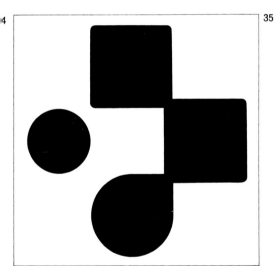

35

37

36

The fact that the elements of the visual are periodic, and that the periodic is an essential part of programming, finds its confirmation here: a photograph put together from photographs. The car is photographed from different angles, the positions of the camera being fixed periodically in accordance with a certain programme. The effect is an imaginary movement in two dimensions at the same time.

The periodic applies not only to the perceptible but also to perception itself, to sensory experience. True, our experience of the world is mediated to us through only two eyes, but our eyes are constantly moving in our head, with our head and with our body. That is the experience of space and time which (mortals that we are) we apprehend as being continuous.

Which is another point I wanted to make: the picture is a good illustration of the problems raised in this book. To see a thing in various perspectives; to select the viewpoints so that the views (cumulatively) produce a new whole. In the illustration below a programme has been made out of this approach, and as far as the book is concerned, a virtue has been made out of necessity.

Designing programmes: why is it so difficult to define what is meant in a nutshell. The subtitle: instead of solutions for problems programmes for solutions is more exact, certainly, but scarcely more graphic. The position is probably this: there can be no clear concept of something which, while not new, is not yet firmly fixed in the conscious mind; that is to say, which is still unclear in itself. This introduction, Gredinger's introduction, the whole book is nothing but a definition in different perspectives. Perhaps the title will take on substance as the reader goes through the text. Perhaps the words will become a concept? That would be ideal.

38

Again: Programme as Photography

The photograph below shows what might be termed a metaphysical view of the same object, viz. a car. It is an extract from a "pastework picture" by Vera Spoerri.

"No one has yet seen a table as it really is", says the mathematician Andreas Speiser, "but always only a part view relative to the point from which it is viewed. The table itself is an unalterable object which constantly appears in a variety of aspects. It is therefore an invariant, an unalterable, in an infinite number of pictures. Let us remember this law: in the apparently unordered sequence of our visual ideas appear invariant structures, these very objects in space; these ideas are by no means voluntary but linked through the operation of a law with existing objects, they are conditioned by something absolute and therefore relative to this. Mathematics can create such relations a priori, and the theory of relativity is born, but it is actually an invariant theory."

However much this picture may differ from the picture on the left, the differences between the two underlying programmes are small. Thus: on the left is the full view of the car, here are parts of the car photographed from periodically fixed viewpoints and pieced together. In both cases the points from which the car is viewed are virtually the same; the distances away are different: farther away on the left, closer here. In both cases the beholder sees different views of the body – from in front, from the side, from above – in the flat. That is to say, what is in reality perceived spatially only at different points of time is here experienced simultaneously.

(Perhaps it may even be possible to bring off the trick of not only showing a full view of the car from outside but also doing away with the contrast of inside and outside. The camera would not merely wander round the object but through it. It is the same principle as the Möbius band. It is a question of programming.)

Programme as literature
Programme for Berio
by Markus Kutter

It came about like this:

In his arm-chair on the balcony at Hegenheim (or over a glass in a hotel?) Berio asked whether the lyrics writer could not write lyrics like this:

Few words.
Simple words.
But words which could be sung back-to-front and front-to-back.
Or even over one another.
Or higgledy-piggledy.
Or, of course, after one another.
Now just a few words picked out.
Now one beautiful word alone.
Perhaps a long chain in which the links are continually rearranged.
And it must make sense.
And it must have atmosphere and sound marvellous.

For example, for a woman's voice.
(Because his wife Kathie sings so well).
And so the lyrics writer had to try to write lyrics.
Difficulty: the lyrics writer can only write with confidence in German. But the lyrics must be translatable, for example into English. So they must not be complicated.
The text scheme produced is at the foot of this page.
This programme can be used in the following sequences:

Sequence a b c d e f g h i
or e alone
or a e i
or a d g b e h c f i
or g h i a b c f e d
or a d e f i
or c f i a d g h e b
or c e g

or any sequence one cares to choose.
I hope Berio will compose the programme before long;
I should like to hear it – because of Kathie's beautiful voice!

a	b	c
Give me	a few words	for a woman
d	**e**	**f**
to sing	a truth	that allows us
g	**h**	**i**
before night falls	without sorrow	to build a house

Programme as music

Variations I
by John Cage
for David Tudor, on his birthday (tardily), January 1958

Six squares of transparent material, one having points of 4 sizes: the 13 very small ones are single sounds; the 7 small but larger ones are 2 sounds; the 3 of greater size are 3 sounds; the 4 largest 4 or more sounds. Pluralities are played together or as "constellations". In using pluralities, an equal number of the 5 other squares (having 5 lines each) are to be used for determinations, or equal number of positions, – each square having 4.

The 5 lines are: lowest frequency, simplest overtone structure, greatest amplitude, least duration, and earliest occurence within a decided upon time. Perpendiculars from points to lines give distances to be measured or simply observed. Any number of performers; any kind and number of instruments. J.C.

Figs:
41 the square with dots, 42 one of the 5 squares with 5 lines, 43 the lined square placed over the dotted square and 44, the dots connected by perpendiculars to one of the lines.

41
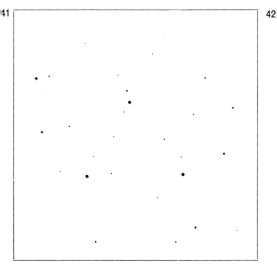

42
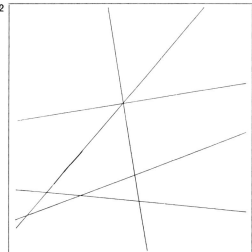

43
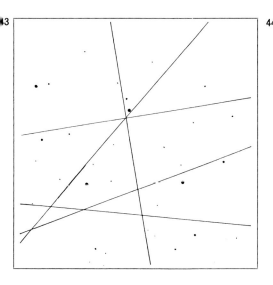

44
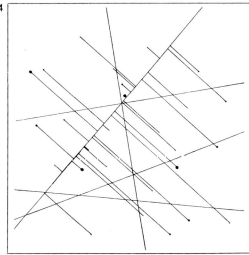

The old Berthold sans-serif on a new basis

Many ask: Is there a future for sans-serif as a type-face?

There is no doubt that it is being used on an increasing scale. But two interpretations can be placed upon this fact.

Some say: sans-serif has become a vogue which will go out again (like the boom).

Others say: sans-serif began as a face for accentuation but is now a body type (just as black letter, old face and roman were for decades, if not centuries).

I side with the others. I do not mean by this that the modern designer must regard sans-serif or roman as mutually exclusively alternatives. We have progressed beyond the either-or philosophy of the twenties. Today sans-serif v. roman is no more a question of conscience than symmetry v. asymmetry.

It is my conviction that the evolution of typefaces is a long-term question of style and thus at short range (inevitably) a question of fashion.

Style is the adaptation of the forms of function and display to the spirit (and hence to the taste) of the times. From this point of view, the constant change of typefaces affords a text-book example, taking place as it does within limits which allow developments to be viewed as a whole. The function is fixed, the alphabet invented, and the basic forms of the letters are unalterable. Black letter and sans-serif are closer to each other than Ulm Cathedral is to the Thyssen House, with which, however, sans-serif has more stylistic features in common than any other printing type. After all, they both have the same historic roots, for both industrial architecture and sans-serif (the industrial typeface) came from early 19th century Britain.

No doubt sans-serif does not represent the final stage but only an intermediate stage (like every other face).

No doubt a thousand other variants will be derived from the roman-humanistic alphabet. But the new types will not be those of the past.

As I interpret the present situation, taking the past as my yardstick, sans-serif not only has a future, it is the typeface of the future.

When we say sans-serif, we are referring to a specific form of the alphabet in which the letters have no serifs. But there is no one-and-only sans-serif. There are hundreds of forms, each with specific characteristics. There are hundreds of variants of the original, each more or less divergent, each more or less original.

The first question we asked ourselves was: Which of all the sans-serif faces in favour today do we prefer? And then: What criteria are we to apply to typefaces for the typography of today and tomorrow?

Our answer was: Most of the variants are, at best, no worse than their predecessors, but they can only be called improvements with reservations. We prefer the original sans-serif. We hold that, instead of designing new type, we should improve the original faces which have proved best after the test of time (a subtle distinction!). That is the first step. Then secondly we should develop them harmoniously, (i.e. in accordance with a governing principle) and bring them as close as possible to perfection.

This is what we have attempted of our own accord and without prejudice, choosing for the purpose Berthold sans-serif, which after careful comparison we considered the most suitable (We = the staff of Gerstner, Gredinger and Kutter, Advertising Agency, Basle).

The seven sans-serif typefaces most commonly used today

These can be arranged in three groups according to the date of their origin:
1. the original faces devised by practising craftsmen
2. the deliberately stylized faces of the twenties
3. the visually clarified faces of 1957.

The date given is in each case the year in which the cut first appeared. I have, however, included Mono 215 in the first group although it did not come onto the market until 1926. My reason is that it was cut in imitation of various craft models and does not represent the personal achievement of the designer.

The two cuts of the twenties are quite different. Both represent strongly individual contributions to the development of typefaces and bear the stamp of their designers.

The first of these is Futura. Renner was concerned to sever every possible connection with tradition. He designed a face by geometrical rules, using the square, triangle and circle.

Secondly we have Gill. Gill sought to bring his sans-serif as close to tradition as he could. Certainly he did not disdain ruler and compasses in producing his sans-serif, but he was guided by the optical conformity of old face to an inner principle.

Futura 1927	physiognomie
Gill 1927	physiognomie
Univers 1957	physiognomie
Helvetica 1957	physiognomie
Folio 1957	physiognomie
Mono 215 1926	physiognomie
Akzidenz 1898	physiognomie

The cuts of the third group, Univers, Folio and Helvetica, all appeared on the market in 1957. Although they vary in originality and quality, they have more features in common than any other group of sans-serif.

Is this coincidence? – Rather the spirit of the age! Future typographers will speak of the typical cuts of the fifties.

What these faces have in common shows in both the general trend of their style and in their detail.

An example: although these faces are all by well-known designers, the "personal calligraphy" has been deliberately suppressed. There is no marked determination on their part to insist on a personal style.

Here the formal contrasts, which Renner wanted to emphasize, are smoothed out. Unlike Futura and Gill, all these three faces are virtually devoid of geo-metrical elements and have been designed in conformity with optical laws.

This is tantamount to saying that the cuts of 1957 follow along the lines of the original craft faces of the first group. They are variants with delicate differences. The individual letters have a large face, create a restful rhythm in the appearance of the word (note the horizontal ends of the strokes), and produce a uniform grey tone in composition.

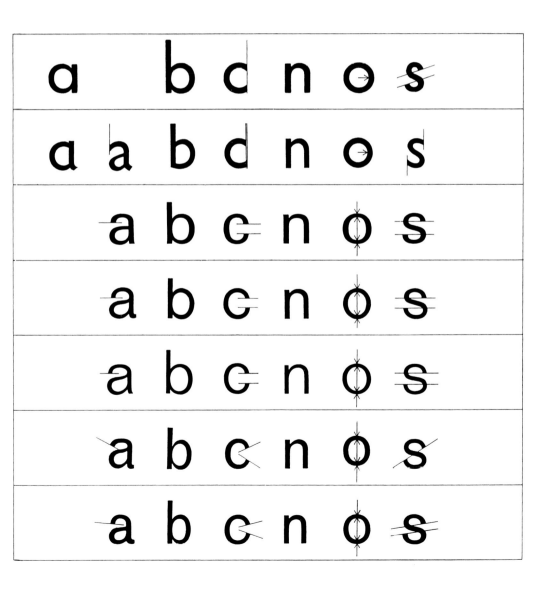

Why do we prefer Berthold sans-serif?

Are the original craft faces like Berthold sans-serif unquiet and unbalanced when compared with the cuts of 1957? It depends on how they are read.

Is it a criterion that the composition should be uniformly grey? Is it a criterion that a face should be as elegant and balanced as possible? Yes. It is a graphic but not a functional criterion. What has ocular clarity may appear monotonous when read.

The quality of sans-serif which is sometimes criticized as "restless" seems to us to be its chief virtue: its vitality, its (literally) original freshness.

Actually, Berthold sans-serif has survived the vagaries of fashion for over sixty years. It is a typeface that was never particularly pushed by the firm that made it. It is a face that has gained acceptance everywhere on its own merits even from designers with the strongest personal convictions, and it goes on from strength to strength.

We will admit that our criteria are not conclusive. The selection of a typeface is always a matter of judgment. But whatever the criteria, Berthold is an outstanding sans-serif!

Aa Bb Cc
Dd Ee Ff Gg
Hh Ii Jj Kk
Ll Mm Nn Oo
Pp Qq Rr Ss
Tt Uu Vv Ww
Xx Yy Zz

To whom is the credit due? Who designed Berthold sans-serif?

The name is unknown. It is the work of anonymous type cutters; that is to say, craftsmen and specialists who through experience and the exercise of their trade knew all about the most subtle aspects of typefaces (not only sans-serif) and the rules to which they conform.

They conferred upon Berthold those self-evident qualities of form and function which have outlived the passing fashion. There can be no higher praise for a typeface.

The know-how of the craftsman is expressed not only in the type letters but also in the composition.

Here is proof. Each individual type size was cut on its own without the use of the pantograph or photo-optical appliances. Each is proportioned to its size in accordance with the rule that the small sizes should have proportionally more width than the larger ones.

We have tested this with founder's type on the market today. We took seven different sizes and scaled them up or down to 36 points:

6·	efghijklmnop
8·	efghijklmnop
12·	efghijklmnop
16·	efghijklmnop
24·	efghijklmnop
36·	efghijklmnop
48·	efghijklmnop

A typeface is more than its form

Certainly, formal criteria (stylistic features and questions of readability) play an important part in determining the appearance of the type. But the matter is rather more complex.

There are also technical questions to be considered. For what processes is a typeface available? Are the faces identical in hand, machine and photocomposition?
Here the verdict on the various sans-serif faces must vary from case to case. (I must confess to an unqualified admiration for the way in which Frutiger has solved the problem in his Univers).

As might be expected from its craft origins, Berthold is at its best in hand composition (and hence in future photocomposition). This is illustrated by another example taken from our investigation.

Apart from slight and fully warranted differences between the various sizes (the proportionally different widths) there are others which have merely become established in popular favour (as for instance the variations of form seen here in the g). Some other irregularities such as the different positioning of the face are peculiarities of the craftsman concerned and there is no discernible reason for them.

From top to bottom there are four different sizes of print all shown in the same point size; and from left to right the same sizes are shown with the letters all equal in height:

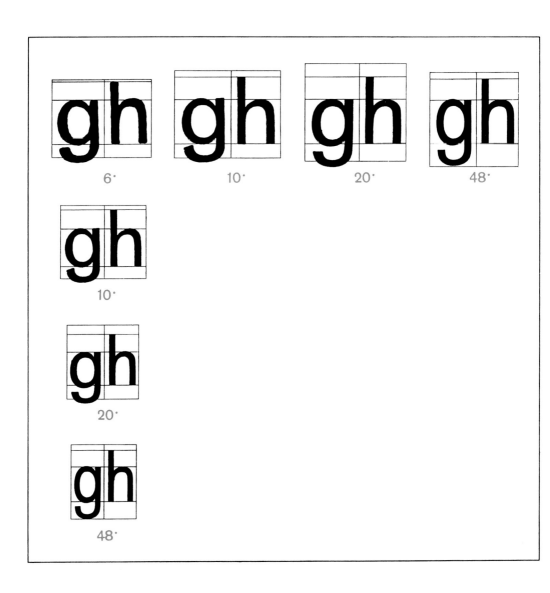

Additional criteria are needed before a verdict can be reached. How developed is a typeface? How many sorts are there and to what extent are these sorts harmonized?

Today these questions are important for the designer, and tomorrow their importance will be greater still. Sans-serif cuts are showing a definite tendency towards more extensive development.

What is the position with the Berthold version? Sixteen sorts have been cut. Some of them (the semibold faces) have become world-famous whereas others have almost been forgotten, some with good reason and others (the light and the condensed light) with less justification.

Each of the four degrees of boldness ranks in its own right among the outstanding cuts.

However, the strongly individual character of the cuts does have one inevitable disadvantage, and that is that they are not easy to combine in the accentuated sizes. Differing as they do in the length of their ascenders and descenders, the letters cannot keep in line. (But it would be a mistake to imagine that sorts have necessarily been harmonized once this desideratum has been satisfied). The 4 degrees of boldness of 20-point size:

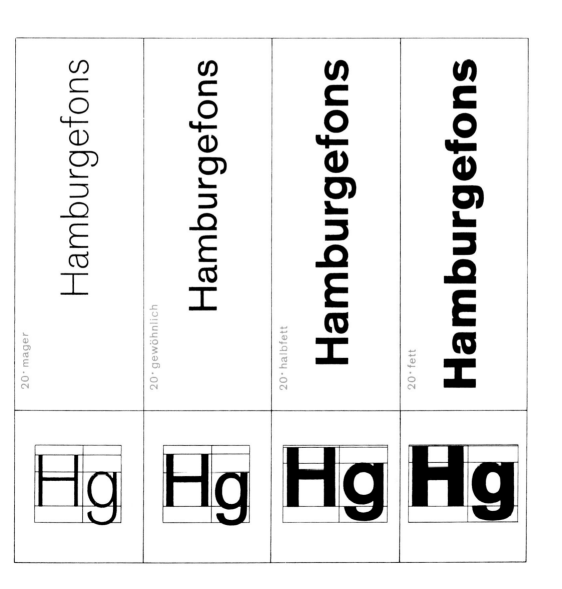

Before we could extend the old Berthold sans-serif to form a new and harmonious family of typefaces, we had to find a basis. We had to decide which face to take as a basic type from which the variants could be derived. For this purpose we chose the standard type in the Diatype version made under the direction of Günter Gerhard Lange. Moreover, we took some of the capitals (BDEFGKPR) and made some slight modifications (see p. 22). As regards technical questions, we assumed that photocomposition was being used.

In principle the basic type can be changed in four different ways:

1. large–small
2. narrow–wide
3. lean–fat
4. roman–italic

The first three parameters comprise sequences which are theoretically infinite but limits are, of course, set to them in practice. There is an upward limit to size and certainly a downward one, a limit to narrowness and width, a limit to leanness and fatness. Within these sequences there are reasonable bounds; extremes set by technical and functional experience.

However, there are any number of degrees within these extremes. After the first decision (what are the extremes) there is a second one to be made:
how many different sizes
how many different widths
how many different degrees of fatness between the extremes?

The first question as to size provides its own answer. It is left to the judgment of the user. It is of capital importance for designing with the typeface but not for designing the typeface itself. The question as to fatness and width is rather different. How many degrees are reasonable? The intervals should be reasonably small so as not to forfeit continuity, but also reasonably large so that the various degrees can be readily distinguished. We decided on four of each.

There follows the third decision: on what basis is the design to rest?
a) what principle and
b) what factor?
These questions are central. On the answers depends the success of our programme, which is to ensure that each sort should combine harmoniously with the others. In this context "harmonious" means that there must be exact concord between the variants by reason of the intrinsic law that governs them and not merely an external similarity derived from convention.

Finally a word about the fourth parameter: roman–italic. Every fully developed typeface has an italic as a companion to its roman form. It is the oldest form of variant face there is and began, to the best of my knowledge, with Caslon. Hitherto roman and italic have always been considered as alternatives, as a pair. Now, if this parameter is considered under the more general aspect of inclination, it will acquire a different importance. For the upright–the 90° to the horizontal–is merely a special case of inclination. I shall revert to this on page 31.

1. Large–small

The principle adopted is that of making a variable quantity of the radius of the letter measured from an imaginary centre. This means that height, width and fatness increase or decrease as the case may be. The letter becomes proportionally smaller or larger.

This principle finds application in photocomposition. The letters are projected. Each size, of course, imposes its own optical conditions. What the cutter corrected beforehand in the form (see p. 23) is now regulated by the Diatype machine in the ductus. That is to say, the letters are not broadened downward but the spacing is made larger.

Here is an illustration. 48 points: first line in photocomposition, second line in hand composition. 6 points: first line 48 points photocomposition reduced just as it is, second line corrected in the ductus, third line hand set. 12 and 24 points likewise.

In hand and machine composition how large or small the letters are depends on the size of the type. In photocomposition the size can be varied at will (not in every process but at least with the Diatype machine). Here the designer can determine the factor. That is to say, if he uses different sizes for the same printed matter, he can fix precisely what relations he likes between them.

48·	efghijklmnop
	efghijklmnop

6·	efghijklmnop
	efghijklmnop
	efghijklmnop

12·	efghijklmnop
	efghijklmnop
	efghijklmnop

24·	efghijklmnop
	efghijklmnop
	efghijklmnop

2. Narrow–wide

Principle: the variable quantity is the horizontal axis of the letter.

That is to say, all the dimensions become proportionally larger along this axis whereas the vertical dimensions remain unchanged. The letter becomes wider or narrower.

The basic type bb is narrowed once, producing ba, and widened twice, producing bc and bd.

It is now important to introduce a factor which will fix these two degrees in conformity with a rule. This factor is 1.25. That is to say, ba is related to bb as 1 is to 1.25. Furthermore: bb is related to ba as bc is to bb, and so forth.

At the same time the letter is automatically broadened as a whole: the ratio of the stroke to the counter remains the same in all widths. The form remains unchanged.

In other words, not only the width changes but also the thickness of the strokes. I shall revert to the importance of this point on page 30.

ba	ba
Hamburgefons	O
bb	**bb**
Hamburgefons	O
bc	**bc**
Hamburgefons	O
bd	**bd**
Hamburgefons	O

3. Lean–fat

Principle: the variable quantity is the thickness of the stroke of the letter.

That is to say, the letter becomes proportionally leaner or fatter (in relation to its thinnest and thickest part).

The basic type bb is diminished once (ab) and broadened twice (cb, db).

The factor is the same as that used in widening the letter, i.e. 1.25. That is to say, ab is related to bb as 1:1.25. bb is related to ab as cb to bb and so forth. At the same time the letter becomes not only fatter or leaner, but also wider or higher. This difference of height can be corrected at will by means of the infinitely variable adjustment of size possible with the Diatype machine.

ab	ab
Hamburgefons	O
bb	bb
Hamburgefons	O
cb	cb
Hamburgefons	O
db	db
Hamburgefons	O

The System

Degrees of fatness and width are harmoniously co-ordinated by the common factor. For this reason it is possible to arrange them in a kind of co-ordinate frame and to add others to them.

That is to say, the four degrees of width ba–bb–bc–bd are arranged horizontally and the four degrees of fatness ab–bb–cb–db vertically round the basic type bb as the intersecting point. Starting from this cross, the remaining fields can be filled in: the missing sorts follow automatically.

The system is a complex one and reveals a new relationship: all the sorts along the same diagonal are of different widths but of equal fatness. Not only the horizontal and vertical rows display a constant relationship but also the diagonals ba–ab, ca–bb–ac, da–cb–bc–ad, db–cc–bd, dc–cd.

These 5 diagonal rows are terminated at one end by the lean-narrow extreme aa and at the other end by the fat-wide extreme dd. The system is also complete. It is impossible to draw the face in a more extreme form in either direction without abandoning the basic form and the basic principle of proportional change, which would render the system nugatory.

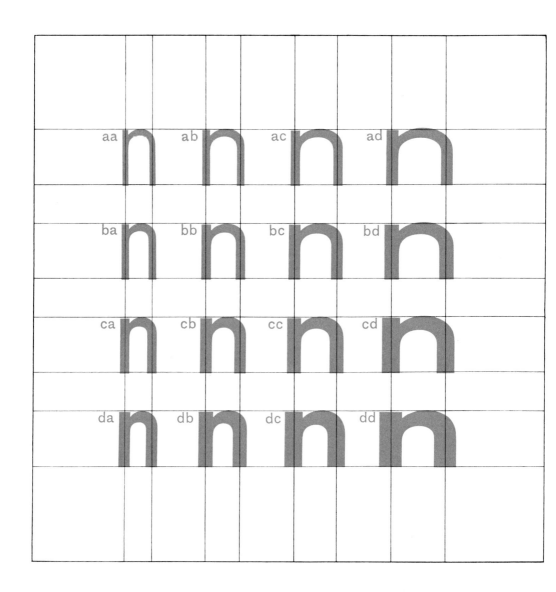

4. Roman–italic

Principle: the variable quantity is the angle between the vertical and horizontal axes of the letter.

That is to say, width, height and thickness of strokes remain constant. The letter is tilted forwards or backwards at a greater or lesser angle.

It is also to the point to ask: how many angles of inclination are rational? We might adopt the same ratio of 3:4 for the inclination as we used for the changes in the width and fatness. Taking a perpendicular in place of the basic type bb, we should have a left-sloping italic of 80 degrees on the one hand, and two right-sloping italics of 80 and 71.1 degrees on the other.

It is too early, however, to consider this yet. One day such forms will come into being, but at present there are no typographical criteria and the technical facilities are not available.

For this reason we have merely produced the 16 sorts in a proportional italic forming an angle of 78 degrees to the horizontal. That is to say, we have transferred the form unchanged to a parallelogram with a base angle of 78 degrees.

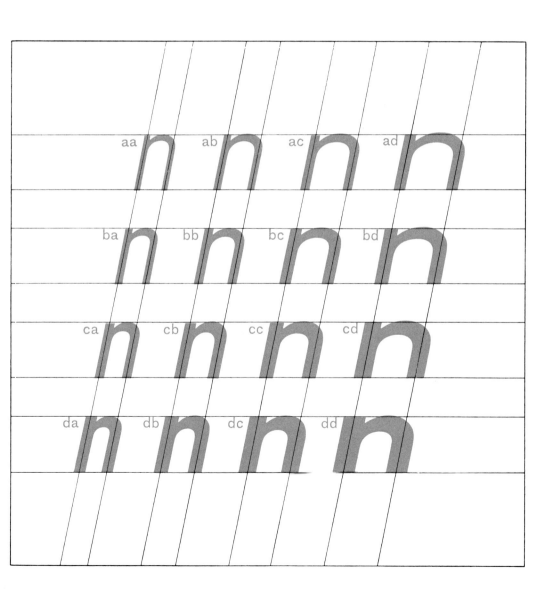

Hamburgefons

Hamburgefons

Hamburgefons

Hamburgefons

Hamburgefons

Hamburgefons

Hamburgefons

Hamburgefons

Hamburgefons

Hamburgefons

Hamburgefons

Hamburgefons

Hamburgefons

Hamburgefons

Hamburgefons

Hamburgefons

Hamburgefons

Hamburgefons

Hamburgefons

Hamburgefons

Hamburgefons

Hamburgefons

Hamburgefons

Hamburgefons

While engaged in this work, we were sometimes asked whether we were not proceeding on rather too rigid lines.

I think there is a misunderstanding implicit in such a question. It is true we looked for a scheme. But by scheme we do not mean making a decision and then carrying it out regardless of consequences. What we wanted was that both the single type and the whole family should conform optimally to a governing principle. Looking at it like that, we cannot be schematic enough.

We went ahead on entirely conventional lines. We slowly passed over from analysis to synthesis. By analysing existing typefaces, we learnt what we could discard. The synthesis was approached by trial and error in a hundred different attempts. Step by step we measured our abstract ideas (the principles we evolved) against the result, i.e. the actual appearance of the typeface. In principle we now know what we want. But we also know that there still remains a great deal to be done in detail. Let me repeat our principle: not to design new faces but to improve (where possible) and to develop the best, perfecting them to the utmost and making them conform to a governing principle as far as possible.

Why is this conformation to a governing principle so important? Because we set such store by being able to combine the letters harmoniously and without restriction. But is the typographer not free to combine as he likes? No, all he can do is combine the material available. And in our opinion that is too little.

Perhaps I may be permitted a personal observation. In the future there may be a closer link between text and typography, between content and form. Certainly there will be in advertising, probably in journalism, and perhaps in literature.

As the flood of printed matter grows in volume, copy writers and typographers must look for ways and means of making what is printed easier to read. The typeface is the medium of communication and typography is the packing. The face must be legible but the typography must make the print inviting. This function is very important, and the typography can fulfil it in a variety of ways.

But there must also be more variety in the material. There must be variety but in our view there must also be a strict constant. That is the new basis we want for the old Berthold sans-serif.

We in our agency are primarily typographers not "typeface artists". It was never our intention to design a new typeface. Quite apart from that, we did not originally even aspire to do the work I am here presenting to a professional public for the first time. It has given us enjoyment because tackling these problems has given us a sharper eye and a deeper understanding not only of typefaces but also of the typography of the future.

It will soon be three years since we first began this work. It gives me pleasure to record that when our work began to yield results we approached the firm of Berthold. The management and artistic director showed sympathetic interest in what we were doing. Berthold provided a tangible basis for our work and have assured us that they will be bringing out this new design in photocomposition on Diatype.

Basel, february 1963

Integral typography

A new label? The typographical aspect of a new ism?
No, this is just what is not meant. The times of both,
pioneers and isms, are over. After the adventurers of
the 'teens and the twenties we are the settlers, the
colonizers.

The continent of modern creation is not only discovered, but it already figures on various maps. Isms are
the countries of the spiritual map, each one with a
border separating it from the others as in a school
geography – and like everything in school books right
and wrong at the same time. For today the border-
lines between isms are beginning to be obscured.
And what interest us are not so much the surround-
ing constructions as the matter itself, the individual
achievement which stands finally behind collective
theories. In my opinion, for the sake of honesty, no
new ism should be created[1].

Today it is time (at any rate so it seems to me) to gain
distance from the theses of the "new" and "elementary" typography of the twenties and the "functional"
typography of the early forties.

Let us recapitulate these theses once again. Max Bill
writes in 1946: "We call elementary typography a
typography entirely developed out of its own data;
that is to say, which works in an elementary way with
basic typographical elements, and if, at the same
time, it aims at the sentence-picture in such a way
that it becomes a living sentence-organism without
any decorative addition and without any strain, we
would call it functional or organic typography. Which
is to say that all demands – technical, economic,
functional and aesthetic – should be fulfilled and
should determine together the sentence-picture[2]."

It is precisely in typography that the difficulty of setting theoretical boundaries is plain[3]. For example dis-
cussing Bill's functional claim, Jan Tschichold, the
editor of "Elementary Typography"[4] said even in
1928: "The New Typography is different from the earlier because it is the first to attempt the derivation of
the appearance from the function of the text[5]." And
Moholy Nagy even five years earlier: "This first of all:
an unambiguous clarity in all typographical works.
Legibility and communication should never suffer
from a previously held aesthetic[6]."

Those were the theses which caused the typographical
revolution and let loose discussion forty, twenty and
even ten years ago. Today it can be said that they are
no longer controversial; they are accepted – and thus
they have lost their object, their currency. This is what
is up to date in the situation of the new typography of
1959. After all a dream has been fulfilled, but the en-
visaged paradise has remained as far away as ever.
In the twenties for instance it was claimed for the
first time that the typographer should proceed from
the data of his material, from the basic typographical
elements; today it is hardly conceivable that he should
not proceed from them.

If most of the pioneers' theses have become self-
evident, the aesthetic criteria have been generally
outlived. For example: Is sans serif or Roman type
the type of the twentieth century (Tschichold 1928:

"Among all existing types the sans serif . . . is the only one which conforms spiritually to our time[5]")? is symmetrical or asymmetrical typography the genuine, contemporary way of expression? do flush left, ragged right or flush left, flush right correspond to present-day feelings? can a type be set vertically or not? and so on.

Such "either or" criteria have served their time and their purpose. Today typographers use both sans serif and Roman type, set books both symmetrically and asymmetrically, use both flush left, ragged right and flush left, flush right. Today everything is stylistically allowable, allowable from the point of view of up-to-dateness. "There remain only open doors to be unlocked", as the German saying has it. And we shall not be spared the necessity of rendering an account of the state of our spiritual inheritance. Nobody will relieve us of the task of searching for new criteria.

Typography is an art not in spite of its serving a purpose but for that very reason. The designer's freedom lies not at the margin of a task but at its very centre. Only then is the typographer free to perform as an artist when he understands and ponders his task in all its parts. And every solution he finds on this basis will be an integral one, will achieve a unity between language and type, between content and form.

Integral means: shaped into a whole. There the Aristotelian dictum that the whole is greater than the sum of its parts is assumed. And this vitally concerns typography. Typography is the art of making a whole out of predetermined parts. The typographer "sets". He sets individual letters into words, words into sentences.

Letters are the elementary particles of the written language – and thus of typography. They are figurative signs for sounds without content, parts which acquire a meaning and a value only if they are combined. This means that combinations of two, three and more letters show in any case a word-picture, but definite letters render a definite idea only in a certain sequence; literally they constitute a word. To clarify the example from the other angle let us take four letters which can be combined in four different ways. From this we can see that only one combination makes sense. The 23 remaining are indeed both legible and pronounceable, they contain the same elements and give the same total. But they do not constitute a linguistic whole. They remain meaningless.

1

EFIW	FEIW	IEFW	WEFI
EFWI	FEWI	IEWF	WEIF
EIFW	FIEW	IFEW	WFEI
EIWF	FIWE	IFWE	WFIE
EWFI	FWEI	IWEF	WIEF
EWIF	FWIE	IWFE	WIFE

The importance of the whole, the integral in general, for language and typography, is obvious. If the proportion between the correct and the possible combinations in words of four letters is 1 : 24, in five-letter words it will be 1 : 120, in six-letter words 1 : 720, in seven-letter words 1 : 5040 and so on.

This means that what we can write and set with our letters in all languages – if it makes sense, it makes a whole – always remains a mere fraction of the mathematical possibilities of the alphabet.

Morgenstern, the Dadaists, Schwitters and others have tried the abstract language which stands for nothing outside itself, consisting of unconventional combinations of sounds and letters, of words which are not words because they have no meaning but their own acoustic and visual rhythm[7]. The poets explode what has become natural and meaningless for us in the language. And in so doing they give us back a feeling for the natural and elementary. Kurt Schwitters' "Sonata in Primeval Sounds" is especially illuminating with respect to the accord between elementary, linguistic and typographical form.

The author says: "The Sonata consists of four movements, an introduction, a coda and a cadenza in the fourth movement. The first movement is a rondo with four main elements which are especially marked in this text of the Sonata. It is rhythm in strong and weak, loud and soft, compressed and extended and so on."

Page 1 of the "Sonata in Primeval Sounds" published in Hannover in 1932. (Typography by Jan Tschichold):

In our contemporary reality abstract word-creations which seem at first sight the eccentric ideas of a poet, have developed into an everyday economic factor. Every day new words are created. Perhaps they grow out of abreviations like UNO, are pieced together from foreign words like Ovomaltine, or are new inventions like Persil; in each case they are independent of their source. And now names for industrial products are found by means of electronic computers. This happens as follows: some three random vowels and four consonants are fed into the computer which registers in a few moments thousands of combinations (see above), replacing imagination by mechanical choice. These meaningless word-creations have become indispensable to publicity. The label departments of every firm of importance have dozens of them in stock; before the products exist the name is already registered and protected by law.

Elementary optics correspond to elementary speech sounds, the formal value of the type corresponds to the acoustic value of language. What Schwitters says about his "Sonata in Primeval Sounds", applies, if correspondingly modified, to the next example, an advertisement for the Delft Cable Works designed by Piet Zwart around 1928. It is a rhythm in black and white, large and small, compressed and extended.

2

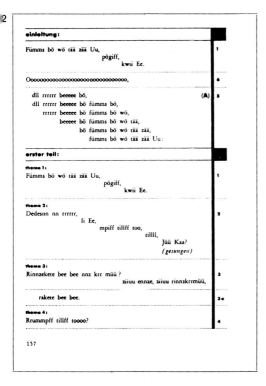

3

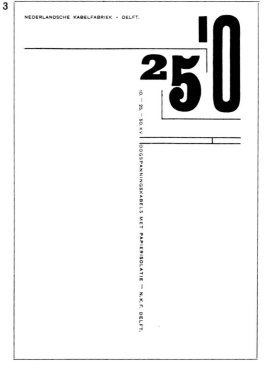

From the point of view of integral typography the illustration below is an interesting example of an influential experiment with fundamentals, though, as its author admits, an imperfect typographical achievement. It is a page of the first printing of Mallarmé's "Coup de dés", published in 1897 in the magazine Cosmopolis[8].

Paul Valéry writes on this[9]: "His (Mallarmé's) whole invention, derived from analyses performed for years on language, books and music, is based on the conception of the page as a visual unity. He had studied very carefully (even on posters and in newspapers) the effect resulting from the distribution of black and white and had compared the intensity of various types ... He creates a surface reading which he combines with the lineal reading, thus enriching the domain of literature with a second dimension." And: "I believe the composition of the "coup de dés" should not be considered as created in two distinct operations, the one consisting in writing a poem in the traditional way, independently of each visual form and the size of the spacing, the other in giving the text its appropriate setting. Mallarmé's attempt must necessarily have been more profound. It happens in the very moment of creation, it is itself a sort of creation."

Mallarmé himself writes in a letter to André Gide: "The poem has just been printed with my sentence-arrangement, in which the whole effect lies." It would not be possible to underline more clearly the relationship existing between the contents and the setting of the text.

If the Schwitters example is a composition of pure type-combinations, Mallarmé's is one of pure word-constellations[10].

The author Eugen Gomringer says: "The constellation, the word-group, replaces the verse. Instead of syntax it is sufficient to allow two, three or more words to achieve their full effect. They seem on the surface without interrelation and sprinkled at random by a careless hand, but looked at more closely, they become the centre of a field of force and define a certain scope. In finding, selecting and putting down these words he creates "thought-objects" and leaves the task of association to the reader, who becomes a collaborator and, in a sense, often the completer of the poem[11]." Further: "Silence distinguishes the new poetry ... in this its prop is the word[12]."

Gomringer calls himself the "play-leader, the one who invites others to play with him". The words he puts down are not words applied to some subject, but a reality, conceptual and rhythmical values in themselves. They are again and again points in relationship to one another in a vacuum in which the reader's imagination wanders, rapidly or leisurely, according to his mood. And the less numerous the points of reference, the more precise they are – which means, in application to typography, the more fixed the unity of word and word-picture, the more natural it is. Lissitzky, addressing the reader, says as early as 1925: "You should demand that the writer take pains over the presentation, because his ideas come to you through the eye and not through the ear. Therefore typographical sculpture, through its visual quality, should do what the speaker's voice does for his thoughts[13]."

4

425

c'était

issu stellaire

le nombre

EXISTÂT-IL
autrement qu'hallucination éparse d'agonie

COMMENÇAT-IL ET CESSÂT-IL
sourdant que nié et clos quand apparu
enfin
par quelque profusion répandue en rareté
SE CHIFFRÂT-IL

évidence de la somme pour peu qu'une
ILLUMINÂT-IL

ce serait

pire
non
davantage ni moins
mais autant indifféremment

LE HASARD

(*Choit*
la plume

5

baum
baum kind

kind
kind hund

hund
hund haus

haus
haus baum

baum kind hund haus

Gomringer also tells us that the poet's distance from the so-called reality of everyday life is at best only apparent. If his constellations are artistically concentrated concentrates, they are often very close to slogans centred on a definite subject, such as: "Cyclists attention-attention cyclists". Or "Face oncoming traffic". Or like the classic among slogans: "Dubo-Dubon-Dubonnet". As publicity for a torch battery the Parisian writer Arman Salacrou conceived: la pile wonder ne s'use que si l'on s'en sert (la pile wonder – the name of the battery – is used up only when in use.)

The newspapers' headlines often become constellations of a particular force[14]. They shape and reduce to the briefest and most direct not only a poetic idea but daily events.

For instance how much is said and at the same time left unsaid in their contemporary context by the four words: Meg to wed court fotog: Princess marries photographer. A subject to excite the imagination of the reading millions. Sensation beyond the scope of normal print. Everyday speech is too elaborate for the headline, too space-consuming. A special solution, then. Abbreviate (fotog); draw upon the thesaurus (wed instead of marries); substitute nicknames (Meg for Margaret). We are interested by the fact that the effect here not only lies in the words, the content of their factual communication. Without any doubt the same words, if they, for example, stood somewhere in the middle pages, would have a completely different effect. Again content and presentation of the language result, cumulatively, in an entirely new unity.

The above examples do not follow any plan and are certainly not intended to be an anthology of pioneer work. I should prefer to look at the theme of integral typography- of the integration of language and type – from as many angles as possible. And there I cannot but mention questions we take for granted. I hope the reader will not consider this too much of a liberty.

We take for granted for instance that on the poster one does not read: "Allianz is organizing an exhibition in the Zurich Museum . . . and so on". The astonishing thing is: nothing is said of an exhibition! The text is reduced to the barest essentials, to names and dates scaled according to their significance – the rest is filled in by the onlooker. Or, in Gomringer's words: "The onlooker completes the poster". The information, though employing only type as its medium, is not as much read as "seen".

Here, using elementary means, the poster fulfils its function in an exemplary way, it conveys its message to the reader in the simplest possible manner, it literally puts him in the picture at the first glance – the information's content and form correspond to one another.

Poster by Max Bill, Zurich 1942:

6

7

"The gravy train
has stopped
running! Let's see
some
action !"

Another phase of integral typography is illustrated by
the following examples. The reader must imagine
what is not shown on the illustrations. Each one is
part of one folder for the New York Times, designed
in 1958 by Louis Silverstein.

"Our
advertising
has to
produce !"

"This is no
time for
**guess-
work !**"

"We've got
to get out
and **sell
sell
sell sell !**"

Have you been hearing these nagging little voices lately? Here's what to do about them:

The mailee receives the prospectus with the figure 8 on the front. He unfolds it, 9, and with each following unfolding, 10 and 11, the size becomes twice as big, the text more insistent and the type heavier. After the dramatic climax "sell sell sell!", – there comes in conclusion the propaganda message – "Put the New York Times Magazine on your magazine schedules . . . use it consistently all year long".

With the elements so far accepted a new one is integrated. The reading-time becomes important, its rhythm is intensified, and it is incorporated into the typographical structure. One can say that text and typography develop simultaneously, as the paper is unfolded. (What is true here for unfolding a sheet of paper can as well be said of turning the pages of a book.)

2

Put **The
New York Times
Magazine**
on your magazine
schedules...use it consistently
all year long

The New York Times folder shows the solution of a complex problem; it displays the integration of an idea, a text and typographical presentation through several phases. It would be a further task to integrate this type of folder with other advertising media or printed matter. Today more than ever, firms need not only a folder here, a poster or an advertisement there. Today something else is needed: a physiognomy, a public face.

The examples on these pages show the physiognomy of "Boîte à musique", a record shop in Basle. "Boîte à musique" has a signature and a style of its own – but not in the sense of an unchangeable mark or of a mere aesthetic principle. Rather do the elements, definitely established though adapted in every case to the functions and proportions, constitute the signature and style in one.

Fig. 13 shows the structure. The lettering and frame are fixed elements; so are the connection between them and the principle of variability. Starting from the bottom right corner, the frame can be increased upward or to the left by whole units at a time. There is no case which is pre-eminent for its proportions. There are only variants of equal value; and the variant is pre-eminent when it is best adapted to the particular problem awaiting solution.

Fig. 14 shows the New Year's card with variants embodying different proportions at one and the same time; 15 the notepaper, in which the insignia is adapted to the (given) DIN A 4 format; 16 and 17 advertisements tailored to fit the advertising space available; 18 a gift voucher.

13

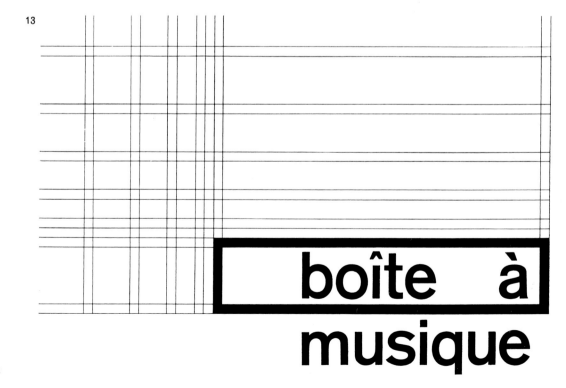

boîte à musique

4

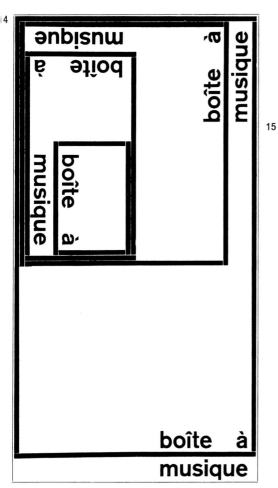

musique
boîte à
boîte à musique
boîte à
musique

boîte à
musique

15

alle platten   bei derrik olsen
im shopping center drachen basel
061 23 04 23
aeschenvorstadt 24

boîte à
musique

6

20 = 1 — das sind
zwanzig schlager auf einer platte
mit dem titel san remo 1958

alle platten — derrik olsen

boîte à

im shopping center drachen basel
23 04 23
über mittag geöffnet

natürlich kennt man edith piaf
doch hinreissender als je ist sie
in ihrem olympia recital.

musique

7

alle platten — derrik olsen
im shopping center drachen basel
23 04 23

boîte à
musique

18

plattenbon

im wert von fr

alle platten bei derrik olsen
im shopping center drachen basel
aeschenvorstadt 24

boîte à
musique

As an addition to Boîte à musique two other cases are quoted which may also be adduced as proof. What is to be shown is the ability of the principle to prove itself in practice; its general applicability first of all with various aids and secondly under various basic conditions.

In the case of Bech Electronic Centre the problem was different only in that the name involved quite different basic conditions. It answers the question Who? (Bech, the proprietor) What? (Electronics, the article) How? (Centre, the type of offer) A description, then, rather than a name; and under the disadvantage of comprising a great deal of text.

I must add that the name does not have this form, as many think, in order to oblige graphic artists. Just the opposite: the design is simply and solely a matter of discerning two characteristics of the name (basic conditions) which lend themselves to the system.

Firstly: the initial letters coincide in the manner of a crossword puzzle when the words are written together so as to read two ways. In other words: the name appears twice without actually being repeated. What appeared a handicap at first, is artificially intensified.

Secondly: the expanded form (horizontal and vertical) contains from the outset variants and combinations. Thus the sign, consisting solely of letters (and without additional aids like the frame in the case of Boîte à musique) can be adapted (within limits) to various proportional requirements. Moreover: through the combinatory variants, it suggests, although not actually interpreting, electronic technique.

Fig. 19 and 20 show the New Year's and also Introductory Card; 19 is the most condensed yet still identifiable form, 20 shows the full range of variability; 21 the firm's notepaper; 22 a repair slip with separable coupon.

19

```
BECH
ELEC
CENT
```

20

```
BECH            BECH           BECH  BEC  BE
ELECTRONIC      ELECTRONIC     LE    ELE  EL
CENTRE              N          EN    CEN  CE
                    T          CT    HCT  HC
                    R          TR    TR    T
                    E          RE    RE    R
                               O     O     O
                               N     N     N
                               I     I     I
                               C     C     C
```

21

R. F. Bech

Zürich
Badenerstrasse 68
Telefon 27 2007 / 233307
Postcheck VIII 23942

- Hochfrequenz- und Elektro-Bauteile
- Apparatebau
- Fernsehtechnik
- Radio- und Grammoabteilung
- Spezialwerkstatt für Reparaturen

**BECH
ELECTRONIC
CENTRE**

HCT
TR
RE
O
N
I
C

Zürich

22

Zürich
Badenerstrasse 68
Telefon 27 2007

BEC
ELE
CEN
HCT
TR
RE
O
N
I
C

Zürich
Badenerstrasse 68
Telefon 27 2007

**BECH
ELECTRONIC
CENTRE**

Fertig bis
Bringen am
Reparaturbericht

Telefon
Artikel
Fehler
Auftrag

Kostenvoranschlag bis
Holen am
Rechnung

3 Monate Garantie auf unsere Arbeit

Werkstattchef

total netto

W L

Diesen Schein benötigen wir wieder, wenn Sie Ihre Reparatur abholen.

Unsere Lagermöglichkeiten sind beschränkt; nach Ablauf von drei Monaten behalten wir uns vor, über nicht abgeholte Reparaturarbeiten anderweitig zu verfügen.

TRONIC
RE

**BECH
ELECTRONIC
CENTRE**
HCT
TR
RE
O
N
I
C

wünscht

von links bis rechts
von oben bis unten
rundum sowohl als auch

ein gutes neues jahr   wünscht

**BECH
E
CH**

E
E
L   ELECTRONIC
E   ECTRONIC
T
R
O
N
I
C

C
CENTRE
T
R
E

BEECH ELECTRONIC CENTRE

Fig. 23 shows the poster in four colours with a sequence from yellow through blue-violet to red, following the movement from horizontal to vertical; 24–26 disc sleeves; 27 an advertisement in the daily press.

24

25

27
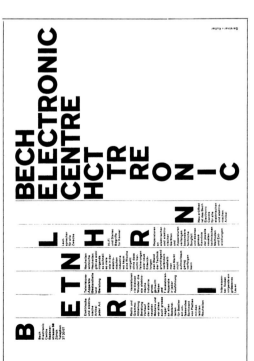

26

With both Boîte à musique and Bech the basic conditions are the same in the way they affect the problem: both are retail shops. In both cases the firm had to be characterized as such and given a physiognomy for the outside world.

In the case of Holzäpfel the structure had an additional task to perform: it had to characterize the products as well as the firm. In other words, a trademark had to be designed in the widest sense of the word.

Vital question: can a mark be variable without at the same time forfeiting its mark-like character? Counterquestion: what is typical about a mark, the proportion or the "configuration"? My answer is known: it is not and cannot be a question merely of proportions as such. Proportions can never be anything but good (or bad) relative to the task. But: in the structure of any sign, however great the number of variants, there is always one which must be declared to be the exemplar. The "configuration" must not suffer as a result of the variability; Fig. 28.

Fig. 29 shows the "printed frame". This characteristic is common to all examples: all consist of parts which are components of the case. There is an economic and also a disciplinary reason for this. Economic because otherwise originals would have to be drawn of every variant of the structure and blocks would have to made of every size. Disciplinary because the typographical units simplify decisions as to proportion from the outset. Fig. 30 is a portion of the system. The thickness of line is the same in all the variants: the size, proportion and boldness are changed. Fig. 31 is a business form; 32 a dispatch label.

28
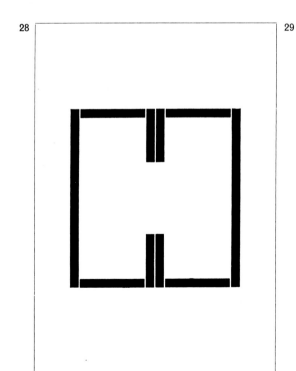

29

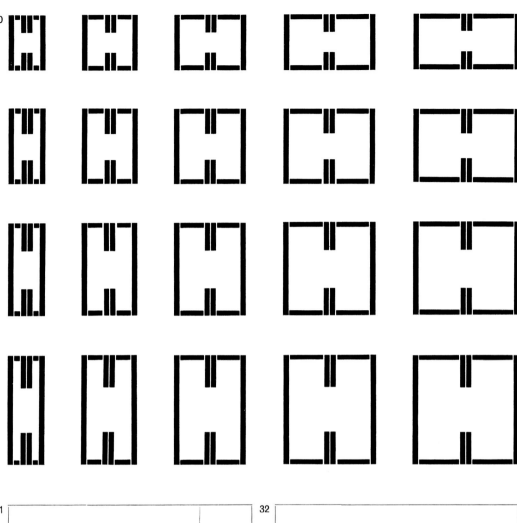

31

32

Christian Holzäpfel KG
Ebhausen Württemberg
Telefon 119/205

Auftrags-Bestätigung

Ihre Bestellung vom diese Nummer bitte bei Schriftwechsel angeben

Ihre Bestellung Nr. Tag

Ihre Kommission Nr. Voraussichtliche Lieferzeit

Vertreter

Versandart

Versandanschrift

wir danken für Ihren Auftrag, den wir zu unseren umseitigen Verkaufs- und Lieferungsbedingungen angenommen haben und wie folgt bestätigen

Pos.	Stück	Bezeichnung	zu DM	DM

Zahlungsbedingungen mit freundlichen Grüßen
Christian Holzäpfel KG

PEN niedriger Schrank

Bezeichnung

Kommissionsnummer

Kunde

Holzäpfel

To pick a variant out of the system and declare it to be a trademark makes sense only where the mark is the sole centre of the item as in examples 33–36. 33 shows the window mark for retailers; 34 a customer giveaway (the sign cast in a perspex cube); 35 matchbook; 36 export mark.

In examples 37–39 the mark is a means to an end. 37 cover for a catalogue. 38 cover for the booklet of instructions for assembling INTERwall – a unit cabinet and partition wall; 39 shows the packing for LIF, an article of furniture for on-the-spot assembly.

33

34

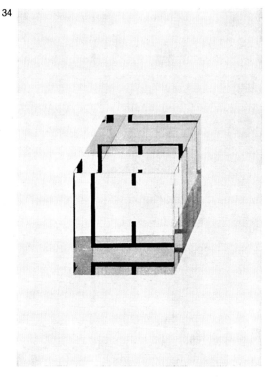

35

36

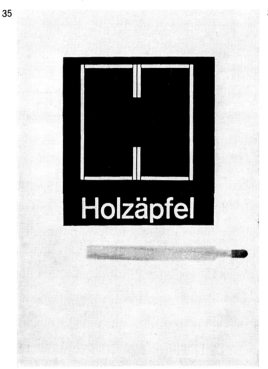

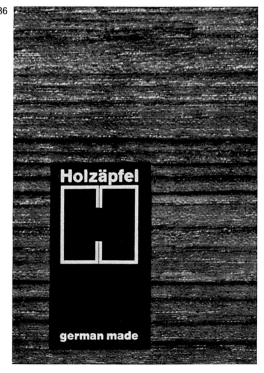

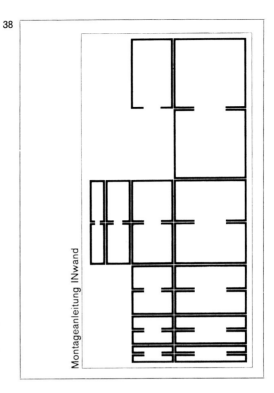

37 Holzäpfel INwand die inwendige Wand in Bau und Haus und Innenraum

38 Montageanleitung INwand

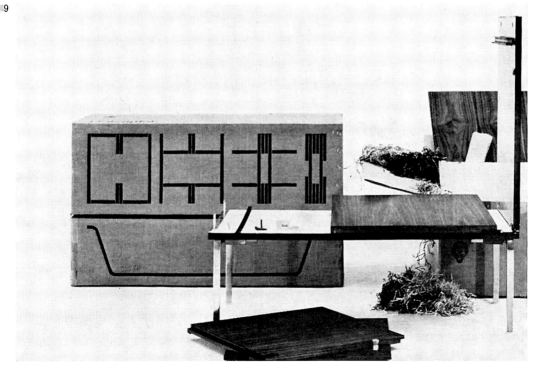

39

Summarized:

1. Integral typography strives for the marriage of language and type resulting in a new unity, in a superior whole. Text and typography are not so much two consecutive processes on different levels as interpenetrating elements.

2. Unity is reached in different phases, each successor including its predecessor:
- in the integration of different signs, different letters into the word. Examples 1 to 4
- in the integration of different words into the sentence. Examples 5 to 8
- in the integration of different sentences into the "reading-time" dimension. Examples 9 to 12
- in the integration of independent problems and functions. Examples 13 to 39.

At the beginning I was rash enough to speak of "searching for new criteria". Has this article been productive of such? Some of the examples cited are old and have already become historic documents. The problems have already arisen and been solved. They have been solved in such a way that the results have remained fresh, living exemplars. Figure 7, the work of Max Bill, for example: If Allianz had to organize an exhibition again, today, twenty years later, the poster might be different but it could scarcely be more pertinent, better, more up to date.

As already said: In essentials these principles of "elementary" and "functional" typography are still valid and are observed to a very great extent. And new ones cannot be added where the solution of single problems is concerned.

However, today there are some changes: the production of printed matter has assumed unforeseen proportions. We are not only threatened by the danger of extravagance and superficiality where the individual creation, however excellent it may be, becomes lost, but also by the menace that the knowledge and experience of the pioneers, what has already been done and is generally recognized, will degenerate into mere formalism, become fashionable. The fulfilment of a dream threatens to become a nightmare. Here we are not allowed to resign. Here the designer must intervene, he must in a sense aim at a larger whole; he must not continue to carry out the single task so much as create structures from which single solutions can be derived.

This adds to the work of design a new dimension of planning, from the angle of both language and type.

The structure, once planned, always contains the elements of text and typography, always comprehends the whole and makes the single task possible. (Consider "Boîte à musique": each task is always typical of the whole, bears the firm's image, and at the same time each is created in view of its special use, from the label to the poster). Thus work becomes more complex, and presupposes an intensified cooperation among all participants. But here design acquires meaning again. The greater effort and longer time dedicated to the development of the structure pays off in the end because it makes the detail work so much easier. And finally the new experience brings forth new impulses for the work on single tasks. In short: From the viewpoint of the whole structure, the integral design itself gains a new stability, a new up- to-dateness, a new significance in this age of short-lived production and corresponding waste of printed matter.

What I have tried to show on these pages cannot be a new typographical style. Because the "New Typography" was not an arbitrary fashion which has now served its purpose. It was the sweeping reform of our most important means of communication, the type face, in a period of sweeping changes. What we can and must do today is not change the inherited principles but extend them to new tasks. From the elementary, from the functional to the structural, the integral: this is the raw material for the new criteria.

Notes on the Essay "Integral Typography".

1

On the isms from 1914–1924 a book by Hans Arp and El Lissitzky appeared: "die Kunst-Ismen". Eugen Rentsch, Erlenbach 1925.

2

From an essay, "über typographie", in "Schweizer Graphische Mitteilungen", May 1946.

3

In other fields than typography the boundaries are more sharply drawn. Georg Schmidt, the apologist of functionalism, writes: "Dutch constructivism acted like a catalyst on architecture and on decorative arts and reduced house, furniture and utensil construction to the most elementary surface, body, space, and material tensions. The result was a much more direct relationship to material and construction in the field of house, furniture, and utensil construction, a complete renouncement of ornament and the discovery of the beauty of 'unornamented form'". But: "Very soon one had to recognize that one had only slipped into a new formalism. Houses and furniture like this tried to be interesting constructivistic sculptures and cared very little for actual use."
"Like every historical error this one was very salutary too. From it arose the further knowledge that house, furniture and utensils are not only conditioned by material and construction like a constructivist picture or a constructivist sculpture but even before this by the function." From an essay "Von der Beziehung zwischen Architektur und Malerei um 1920", in the magazine "Werk", July 1946.

4

"Elementare Typographie" was the title of a special issue of the magazine "Typographische Mitteilungen" edited by Jan Tschichold in Berlin, October 1920.

5

From "Die neue Typographie" by Jan Tschichold, Berlin 1928, Verlag des Bildungsverbandes der Deutschen Buchdrucker.

6

From an essay "Die neue Typographie" from the book "Staatliches Bauhaus in Weimar 1919–1923", Bauhausverlag, Weimar-München 1923.

7

"Die Galgenlieder" by Christian Morgenstern was first published in 1905 by Inselverlag.
To the "Dada" creations in question belong above all Hugo Ball's "Lautgedichte", Hülsenbeck's "Simultangedichte", Raoul Hausmann's phonetic poem "fmsba" which inspired Schwitters, following Hans Bolliger's "Dada-Lexikon", to write his "Sonata in Primeval Sounds". The reader can learn more from the "Dada-Monographie" published by Willy Verkauf, Arthur Niggli, Teufen 1957 and from the "Anthologie des Abseitigen" by Carola Giedion-Welcker, Benteli AG, Bern-Bümpliz 1946.
In a more restricted sense, i.e. rather as artificial than abstract poetry, mention should be made of the recent experimental texts of Max Bense. These texts are pro-

duced mechanically on a basis of aesthetic programming: "Bestandteile des Vorüber" and "Entwurf einer Rheinlandschaft"; both were published by Kiepenheuer and Witsch in Cologne. In 1962 the same publishers brought out Bense's "Theorie der Texte".

8

An excellent edition of the "Coup de dés" was published in accordance with the last directions of the poet, who died in 1897, at the "Librairie Gallimard in "Editions de la Nouvelle Revue Française", Paris 1914. Also in 1897, another poet was giving thought to the typographical presentation of his work: Stefan George. At the "Verlag der Blätter für die Kunst" appeared "Das Jahr der Seele". The typographical design was by Melchior Lechner. In 1898 Arno Holz published the first "Phantasusheft". It contained fifty poems which were free of metrics, strophe, rhyme and were accentuated typographically by the fact that words which belong together rhythmically were always taken together in one line and the lines of most varying length were set on the central axis. A complete edition appeared at J. H. W. Dietz Nachfolger, Berlin 1925. In the following years the poets Apollinaire and Marinetti applied themselves intensely to typography. "Caligrammes" by Apollinaire was published by Gallimard, Paris 1925. Marinetti's principal work in this respect, "Les mots en liberté futuriste", appeared at the "Edizione futurista di poesia", Milan 1919. Besides Schwitters, Käthe Steinitz and Theo van Doesburg ("Die Scheuche", Apossverlag, Hanover 1925) belong to the typographical poet revolutionists. An equally important work is the poetry volume written by Majakowsky and typographically designed by Lissitzky, "Dlja Gôlossa" (to be read aloud), Russian State Edition, Moscow 1923. And so on. A more recent publication in this field is "Les Epiphanies" by Henri Pichette whose typography was designed by Pierre Lefaucheux and appeared 1948 at "k éditeur", Paris. And I may also mention in this ancestors' gallery the novel "Schiff nach Europa" by Markus Kutter, which I organized visually and which was published by Arthur Niggli, Teufen 1957.

9

From the essay on Stéphane Mallarmé in "Variété II", Gallimard, Paris 1930.

10

From "Konstellationen", poetry volume in four languages, Spiral Press, Berne 1953.

11

From an article in "Neue Zürcher Zeitung", September 1954, on the page "Young Swiss Authors answer".

12

From an essay "vom vers zur konstellation, zweck und form einer neuen dichtung", in the magazine "Spirale", No. 5, Spiral Press, Stadion Wankdorf, Berne 1955. "Spirale" publishes in each number authors spiritually related to Gomringer such as Augusto de Campos, Helmut Heissenbüttel, Décio Pignatari and so on. Furthermore Daniel Spoerri publishes a magazine in Darmstadt which counts among its collaborators the same authors as "Spirale". In 1959 there appeared in Sao Paulo at Editora Kos-

mos a volume of constellations, "Poemas", by Theon
Spanudis. The subject of the Integration of Typography in Literature has been treated in numerous
recent publications. Mention may be made of: the
catalogue of the exhibition, "Schrift und Bild" held
in Amsterdam and Baden Baden, 1963; the "Konkrete
Poesie" series, published by Eugen Gomringer himself; Gomringer's own "Konstellationen" collection,
likewise published in Frauenfeld; Markus Kutter's
"Inventar mit 35", brought out in 1961 by Arthur Niggli;
"oddities and curiosities" a delightful collection by
C.C. Bombaugh, published in 1961 by Martin Gardner
at Dover Publication Inc. New York.

[13]

From an article "Typographische Tatsachen" in the
"Gutenberg-Festschrift", Gutenberg-Gesellschaft,
Mainz 1925.

[14]

In another sense André Breton had already made
poetical capital out of this knowledge. With headlines
and headline-fragments cut out of newspapers he
mounted a "Poème" which appeared in "Manifeste
du Surréalisme", Paris 1924. (Published in "Antologia
del Surrealismo" by Carlo Bo, Edizione di Uomo,
Milan 1946.)

Making pictures today?

I will anticipate immediately: I do not know how a
picture of today should look. My criteria are not cut
and dried. In their place I put a number of thoughts
and instead of proofs, comments.

Thoughts and comments related to my personal
activity, an interior and exterior monologue. No programme. An account for me, and maybe (I hope)
a key for the reader. These thoughts would not have
been written down, the comments would not have
been made, without the hospitality of "Spirale",
which I accept with pleasure and gratitude.

Picture-making is one variety, among many, of
design, of invention. The working-area is defined:
the visual field, or more precisely, visual sensation.
The elements are defined: colours. The means are
given: proportions. Thus the craft is: to combine
colours, to fix proportions and to link the two together,
to integrate.

The handling of colours and proportions is based on
experience and grows out of speculation: to have a
feeling for the not-yet-known, to search, to be sur-
prised by what is discovered. Seen as a whole this
means a continuous process whose origin and end
remain obscure. The threshold is given by the picture which, an end-product itself, continuously becomes new experience, a starting-point for the spec-
ulations that follow. To this my contribution may be
original or unoriginal, it may be up-to-date or not.
My contribution may interest the many or the few. As
a designer it is enough for me to apply myself to an
idea. I render this idea concretely in my picture: to
my own order, on my own responsibility, with unlimited liability for the product.

Creation, if understood both as handicraft and spiritual effort, is limited in the first case by my compe-
tence, in the second case by my spiritual standpoint.
In my pictures I can only render and transmit what
represents my own insight into the design of the
world. Andreas Speiser says: ". . . nor is the artist
the creator of his works; he discovers them as does
the mathematician, in a spiritual world created by
god, the only real world . . ."

The up-to-dateness of the picture is one thing, its quality is another. For both there is a binding touchstone – the amount of profit for the onlooker, his momentary and permanent interest. Expressed as a formula: the quality of the picture can be measured by the durability of its up-to-dateness, today and in a hundred years. A good picture always gives back more than the designer could ever put into it; the longer its life, the more it gives. It is indeed created by the designer's intention, but it lives on the onlooker's sympathy.

To take this fact as a working hypothesis means: to have the onlooker participate in the process of design. For instance the "tangential eccentric" is an intentionally unfinished picture; the intention has to be understood as part of the design. I make the choice of the elements and determine the laws of their grouping. The grouping itself, the constellation is "found" by the onlooker. What is important is that if he follows the rules he finds not merely one but x possible completions of the picture, constellations of the same structure which are equal in value, as original as the basic law.

The onlooker changes the picture according to his
disposition and mood. In addition to my intentions –
and perhaps also in spite of them – he invests ideas
of his own. He shares the fun and also the responsibility. He is not a passive admirer but an active partner. As a designer I am convinced that no one is un-
quallfied for this partnership, no one is entirely
untalented, any more than I or anyone else possesses
an unlimited talent.

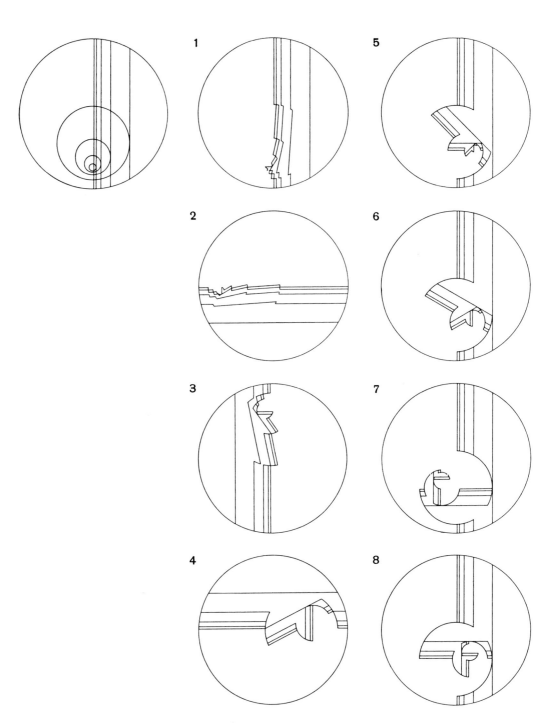

The tangential eccentric: schemes of the basic position and 16 regular constellations.

Five circles, the smaller always within the larger one, are arranged eccentrically on the same axis. Parallel straight-lines are at a tangent to them. Each parallel forms part of a continuous grey sequence from white, the smallest to black, the largest. The circles are movable. The movement interrupts the units of the grey sequence and brings them in each revolving phase into a new aleatory or regular constellation. The regular ones can be obtained by a revolution to left as well as right, with different results, see 7 + 8.

1 Rotation of the circles to right through the smallest unit respectively. Alteration of the basic position through 90° respectively and
2 rotation through the smallest unit to left,
3 through the two smallest units to right,
4 through the three smallest units to right.

5 Rotation of the circles through 45° respectively to left
6 through 60° to left,
7 through 90° to right,
8 through 90° to left,
9 through 180° (the only constellation which cannot be obtained by rotation to right or left).

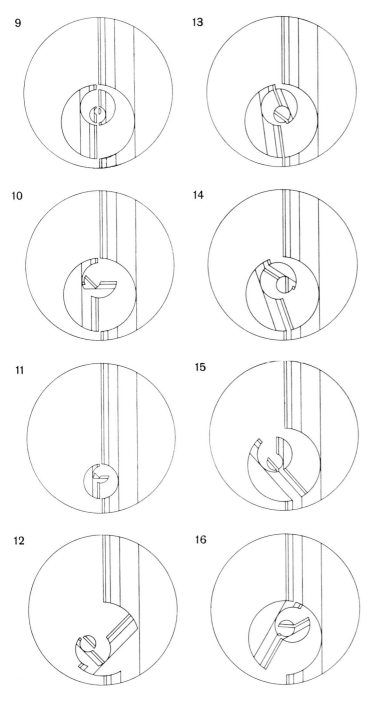

10   progressive rotation through 180°, 90°, 45° to right,
11   through 360°, 180°, 90°, 45° to right,
12   as 10 in inverse order, through 45°, 90°, 180°.

13   rotation not quite 180° to left, each smallest unit
      being joined to its respective opposite end,
14   the second smallest unit joined to its opposite end.

15   rotation of the circles to left, right, left, the third
      respectively joining their opposite ends.
16   rotation of the circles to left, the third, second
      smallest and smallest units respectively joining
      their opposite ends.

Material: peraluman, plastic paint stoved.
Measurements: diameter, 60 cm.

The space–wall–picture 1957–1959, model

To include the onlooker as a future partner in the design of a picture means to operate with an unknown factor. I make the picture dependent on him without knowing who he will be. From this, I hope, an additional tension will arise from the picture to the onlooker. The only facts which I can premise with reference to the onlooker, are of a quantitative, technical nature, if I may say so; a picture for a single person has to be made differently from that for a group. And for the first as well as for the second case there are again certain assumptions: questions of scale and of quality.

Let us take an example in illustration of this: the "tangential eccentric" is created for one person at a time, it is the intimate case of a panel-picture. Whereas the "space-wall-picture" is a picture-panel, so to speak, and is designed for several onlookers at a time. In the first case the onlooker takes part in the design of the picture by moving it, in the second he participates by moving himself. The rest follows: in the "space-wall-picture" the relationship between the picture and the onlooker is governed by the spatial distance.

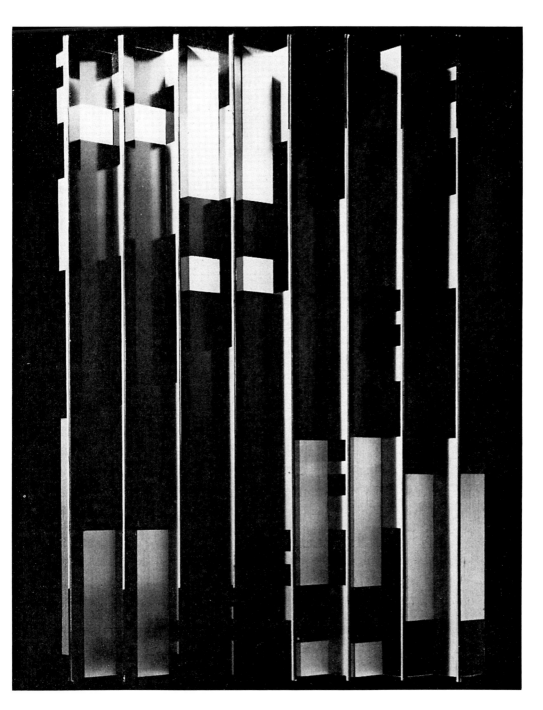

The picture only makes its point in shortened perspective. It is seen by a group of n onlookers, from n different angles of vision, in n different ways. Furthermore, if one, or some, or all members of the group are moving, they are changing, each for himself, not only their position, but at the same time the structure of the picture. And it can never be seen as a whole, it always appears as a constellation of parts. But the parts which are seen at one moment, in their foreshortening, permeation and mixture, automatically form a unity. In other words: from whatever angle it is looked at, the picture appears as much of an entity as its original structure.

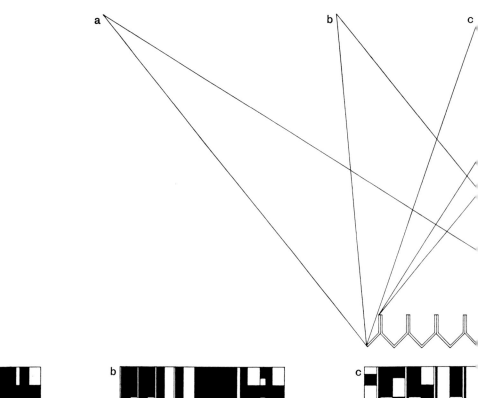

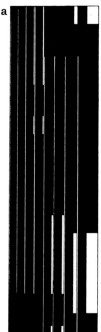

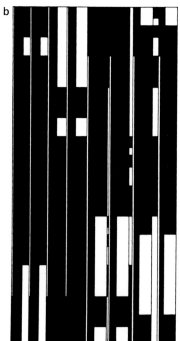

The space-wall-picture: above, plan with the angles of vision a–e; below, drawing of the corresponding views.

The spatial structure, directed to the onlooker, has four planes (the number depends on the picture's structure; in principle it can be reduced to two and extended as desired). The different planes are marked by four groups of eight laminae respectively. The laminae of the first group are divided in the golden section into eight, those of the second into four, those of the third into two units. The units are permutated cyclically; the cycles per group are closed.

The laminae of the fourth group are plain black.

Material: peraluman black and bright, anodized brilliant. The brilliance includes the light as an element of composition. The picture changes with the different phase of daylight, with direct, indirect and artificial light. Moreover the different planes are reflected, the groups seem to interpenetrate. An irrational spatial effect enhances the rational effect and neutralizes it at the same time.

Measurements: height 183 cm, depth of the laminae 9 cm.

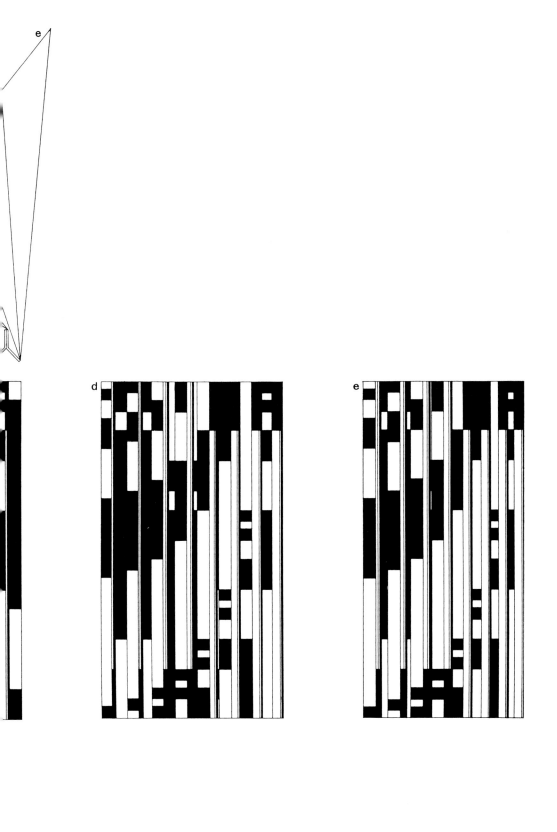

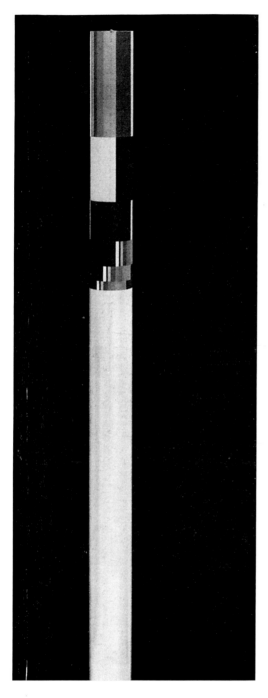

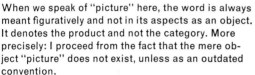

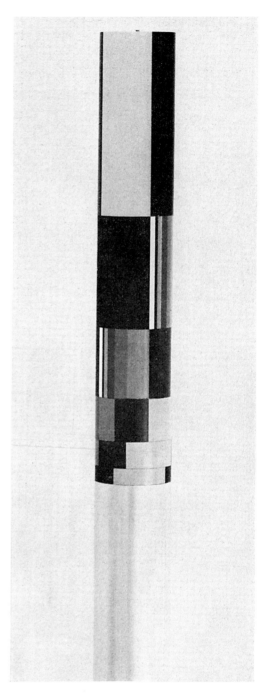

When we speak of "picture" here, the word is always meant figuratively and not in its aspects as an object. It denotes the product and not the category. More precisely: I proceed from the fact that the mere object "picture" does not exist, unless as an outdated convention.

Consequently the picture's outward form cannot be considered as given in advance, but as an integrating part, or rather a result of design.

Outward form means: the picture as material, as body, as mechanism. Picture-formula = picture-object. All parts form a whole from the very beginning, can be considered as a complete entity. This is a method, and what is more, a principle of design. The intention is realized: the totality of all possible relations within the picture. The consequence: the more the single interrelation-ships are differentiated and multiplied, the more the picture as a whole goes beyond the

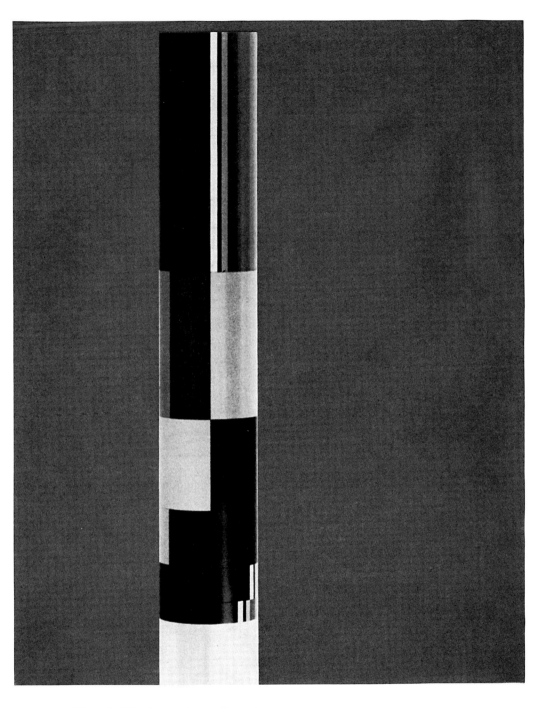

mere sum of its parts; it is also previous to the parts
whose way of appearance is dependent on it. It is
not the result of the summing up, it is its basis.

For example, the "golden sectionized column": it is
not conceivable in any other form than in that of a
column. Its parts can be moved and interchanged. At
the same time, each constellation is different if seen
from different view-points.

1 2 3

The golden sectionized column: pages 64.65, three views of the same constellation; scheme of the basic position and five regular constellations, circumference of the column in projection.

1 Picture-area and foot in the proportion of the golden section. The nine vertical continuous units of the picture-area are in the same proportion. The colours constitute a grey sequence in nine parts which is also continuous; however they are all allotted to the units in such a way that the greatest extremes are placed side by side. In numbers:

succession of the units, ...1 2 3 4 5 6 7 8 9 1...
succession of the grey hues ...1 8 3 6 5 4 7 2 9 1...

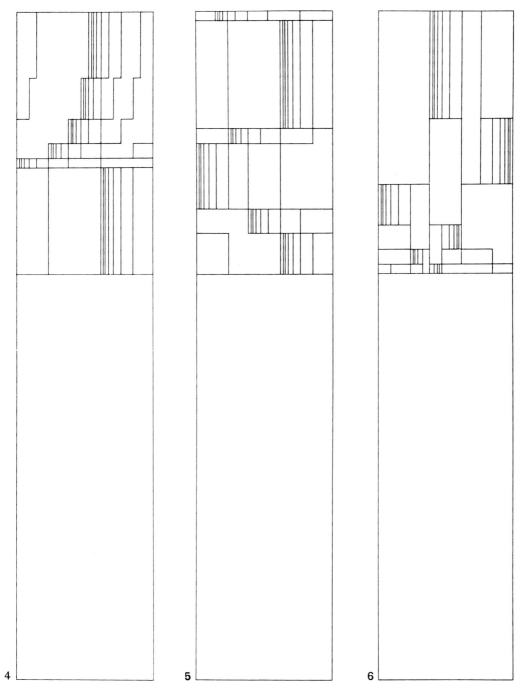

4   5   6

1 = white, 9 = black. From this is apparent a neighbourhood not only of the greatest, 9–1–8, but also of the middle hues, 6–5–4.

2   The verticals are also golden sectionized, horizontally, into single rings; rotation of the rings through three units respectively to right.

3   Progressive rotation from below upwards through 3, 4, 5, 6, 7 units respectively to right.

4   Cyclical permutation in the vertical as well as in the horizontal, obtained by rotating and interchanging the rings.

5   Horizontal-vertical interpenetration obtained in rotating the rings and continuously interchanging them.

6   Reversal through 180° of every second ring. Rotation with reference to the greatest, second, third, fourth and fifth greatest unit.

Material: foot, peraluman anodized bright; picture-area iron tube, plastic paint, stoved.
Measurements: total height 183 cm, height of picture-area 70 cm, diameter 12 cm.

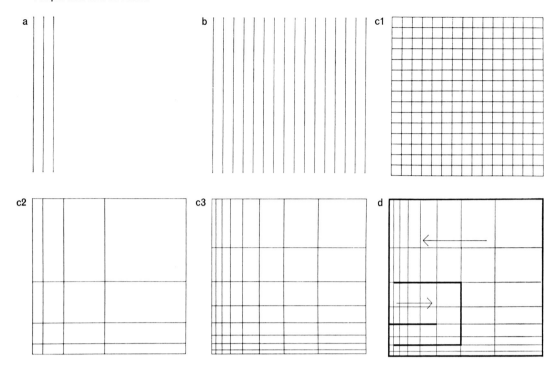

What the examples should illustrate: to plan the functioning of the picture, to set out its relationship to the onlooker, is indirectly part of design. Here follow some thoughts and comments concerning the direct part: the handling of colours and proportions; making out the prescription. Here I proceed from this assumption: there is no hierarchy of the values either of proportion or of colour. Both are media equal in value. The question of harmony or dissonance is one of structure, or in other words, one of the combination of proportion, proportion and colour, colour and colour.

The number of proportions is as unlimited as the numbers themselves, 1000 cases can perhaps be used sensibly, of these I take one:

a   One unit to an equal one, the proportion 1:1, extended into

b, a sequence of 15 units, into

c1, a grid.
    The arithmetical grid c1 is converted into

c2, a geometrical grid in the proportion 1:2
    1:2 divided continuously leads

c3 again into a new proportion within the old; 1: $\sqrt{2}$.
    The grid c3 is the basis for

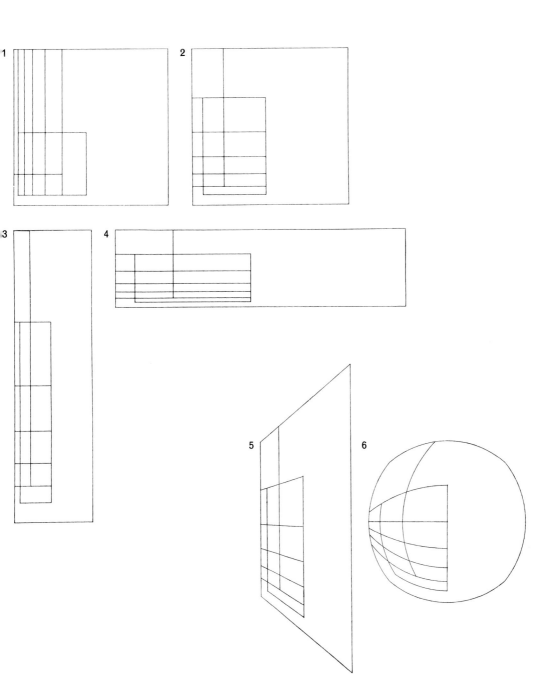

d, the picture-structure: endless movement se-
    quence of a plane by colour transformation.

The structure 1, fixed proportionally, can be changed
proportionally at will. At will = maintaining equal values, though the dimensions change. Some examples:
2   change of the direction of movement on the grid
    c3; the areas of the single fields remain un-
    changed.
3   Change of 2 by changing the basic proportions.
4   Change as 3, in the horizontal.
5   Change by foreshortening.
6   Change by distortion.

The picture-structure is the transition point between
proportion and colour. What is meaningless in the
field of proportions is possible and necessary in handling colours: a system which comprises the totality
of all colours. The richest one I have encountered
is the colour-system of Wilhelm Ostwald (Basic Colour,
an Interpretation of the Ostwald Colour System by
Egbert Jacobson, Paul Theobald, Chicago 1948.)
The representation and designation of the following examples is based on this system.

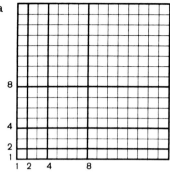

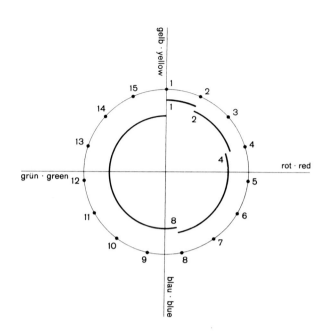

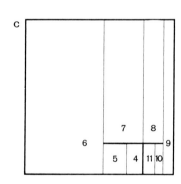

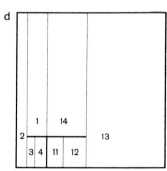

a   Structure and colour correspond to one another. Left, the field of 15 × 15 equal units; right, drawing of the circle of 15 hues with equal distances. The hues of the circle are allotted to the units of the field. For the geometrical grid 1–2–4–8, the corresponding proportions must be carried over on both schemes, (see heavy lines).

b   Colour and structure: endless movement sequence of a field by colour transformations, i.e. after an endless sequence over the circle of 15 hues, hue 1 returns to itself. Function and colour-primacy of example d, page 68, become obvious. The colours can also be interchanged cyclically; each of the 15 hues can be the starting hue without changing the picture essentially.

c   Scheme of the painting "red-green sequence via blue". Red = 4, green = 11. Thus the sequence passes from colour to complementary colour through the blue half of the hue circle. (This picture is no longer based on a hue circle with 15 colours, but on one with 14 colours. For reasons of practical experience I choose for each structure a corresponding division of the hue circle; this is the only deviation from the Ostwald colour system.)

d   = c; the structure is reflected, likewise the colour

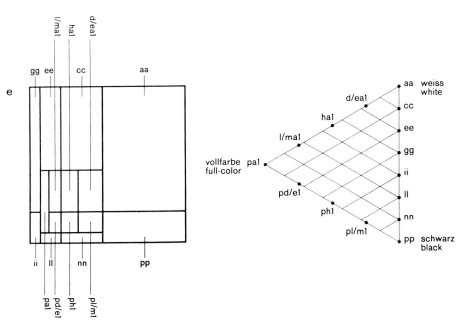

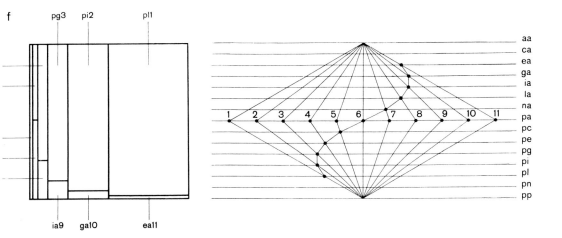

sequence: the hues 4 +11 are the same as in c, at the same place; the sequence however passes through the opposite half of the hue circle, through yellow.

The schemes a–d illustrate simply determined, a + b closed, c + d unclosed–colour sequences on the hue circle. e is an example of a twice-determined closed sequence in the colour triangle, f of a three times determined unclosed sequence on the colour solid.

e   Left side structure scheme of the picture "polar-ized yellow", right side colour sequence in the colour triangle. The full colour pa 1, yellow, is polarized to two sides, to white aa and to black pp.

f   Left side structure scheme of the picture "red to two sides transformed" "twice", right side frontal drawing of the colour solid with 20 full colours, eleven of which are visible. The curve marks the colour sequence: the full colour red pa 6, is trans-formed in twice two directions. On the one hand to yellow hue 1, and blue, hue 11; on the other hand dark-cleared in the direction of black pp until point pl 1, and light-cleared in the direction of white aa until point ea 11.

The picture as design of a whole, a total unity, the unity again thought as a constellation of changeable quantities. This claim involves not only the picture, which, in the end, is actually changeable, but the technique of design in general. The only constant of the picture is its idea; the proportions can be changed, the colours can be interchanged within their system; the measurements are fortuitous.

The claim has its consequences: if all elements of the picture form a whole from the very beginning, they must be freshly fixed for every new picture. i.e. the choice of proportions and colours, of the system of integration, of the dimensions, the position, the material, the construction, the workmanship and so on, re-arises with every new design, according to the idea. Thus the work is a combinatory one; my wish here is: to have not only the most obvious but all combinatory parts at my disposal, a catalogue of all parameters and their elements. Herewith I not only refer to the single solution, complex as it may be, but to the complex of all conceivable solutions in general

Polarized blue 1958/59

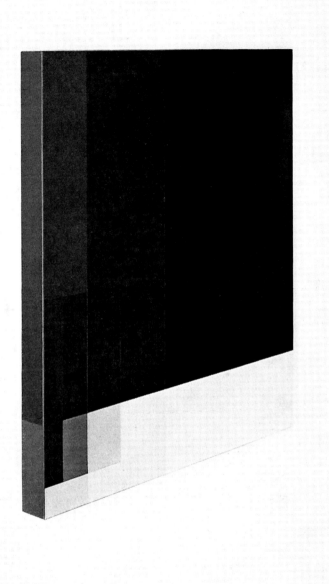

a catalogue of "latent" future pictures. My work as a
designer expressed more precisely: to find among
the innumerable quantity of possible pictures a
number of up-to-date ones. The criterion: the more
universal the formula, the more original is the picture.
The more versatile its unity, or the more uniform its
versatility, the more it can render to the onlooker as
an object of the most personal perceptions.

Alongside the wish the result appears modest. In the
example "polarized yellow" I should like to indicate
just one parameter: the dimension. The colour sequence not only changes direction, but also plane;

from the frontal plane to the lateral plane and back.
Thus firstly the physical dimension of the picture is
fixed: the lateral plane is an integrating part of the
proportional structure; secondly, the intention, the
picture-idea is clarified: without being interrupted
the endless colour sequence is opened between the
black and white poles opposite to the full colour
yellow. Compare page 71, scheme e.

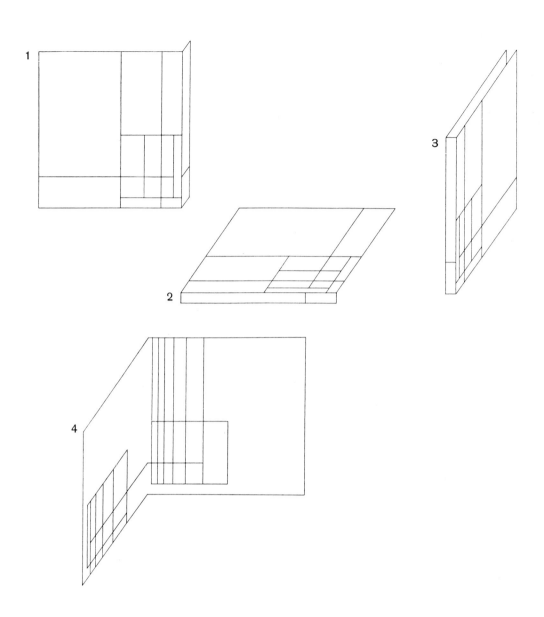

Components of the catalogue of parameters for picture-making illustrated with some examples:

1 Scheme of "polarized yellow". On the pages 72.73 the parameter "dimension" is referred to, and on this page some of the components of "position" are mentioned. The picture, parallel to the wall, in front of the onlooker comes into
2 another relationship with its surroundings; the viewer sees it from above (or below, according to position).
3 The picture is perpendicular to the wall. The on-looker has the view from two or three sides. The structure reflected around the originally lateral plane can also be seen on the opposite side. The colours are reflected too; i.e. the grey sequence remains unchanged, yellow changes into blue, and the steps from full colour to black and white change correspondingly. The frontal narrow plane belongs to the grey sequence common to both sides.

Schemes 1–3 illustrate positions where the affixing of the picture to wall, ceiling or floor is a precondition. Schemes 4–6 contain a further parameter: the body of the picture, which is to be looked at from all sides,

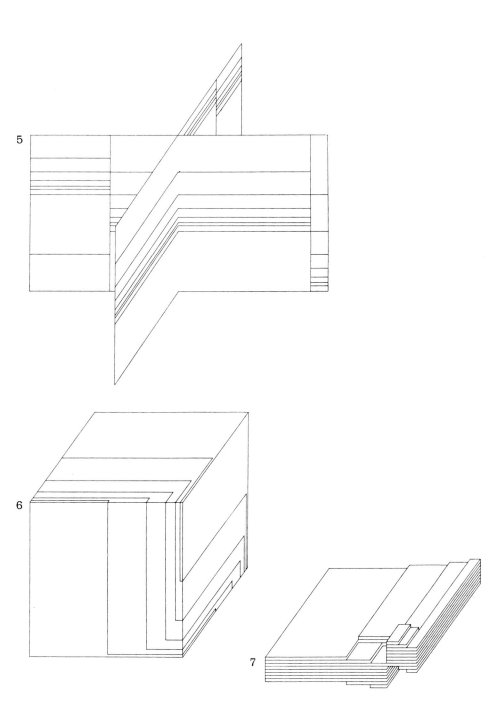

can be stood or laid in any desired position. The
structure integrates spatially-arranged planes into a
whole. Scheme 7 is an illustration of a primarily spatial structure.

4   Two structures (see page 69, schemes 1 | 2) are
    combined and tonally coupled. The coupling be-
    comes apparent from the angular positioning of
    the planes, whereby an inner, and on the reverse
    side a complementary outer, evolution takes place.
5   closed cyclic permutation via the four open inner
    spaces of a cross.
6   Endless colour-movement over the six external

planes of a cube.
7   Spatial version of the picture group "red-green
    sequence via blue" (see page 70, schemes c + d).
    The colour is not merely a surface covering; it
    occupies space itself, in accordance with the
    structure.

Position and body of the picture: components of two
– of how many possible, still to be discovered, parameters? Let us go on making pictures, and find out.

Structure and movement

Four equal sides
four right angles:
one square.

a 1:

Displaced horizontally by the length of one side.
To infinity on the left.
To infinity on the right.

a 2:

The equal areas are distinguished by different shades.
An infinite group of elements.
With terminal limits in black and white.

a 3:

The number of elements
is determined by the gradations between the extremes.
If the gradations are large,
the number of elements is small;
at least two: black and white.
If the gradations are small,
the number will be large; perhaps a thousand,
perhaps the eye can distinguish even more;
probably less.
There are no theoretical limitations:
one shade is darker
than the last even if the gradations are fine,
and vice versa.
Ideally the gradations between successive
shades are equal.
Then the series forms a natural order.

In this case:
a series of 16 equal elements
with 15 equal gradations.
Again, the number of elements is unimportant.
Only the order, the system of reference, is important.

If it forms a whole, self-contained in principle,
we define it as a *structure*.
Movement: means a disturbance of the natural order.

Upsetting the equilibrium of the series;
or giving it a new equilibrium
(which cannot be less complex
than the original structure).
Introducing movement:
starting activity; creating tensions.
Changing the positions of the elements means
giving their relationships new weight,
giving the whole a new appearance.

This implies: creating different effects
with the same elements.
Deriving different constellations
from a single structure.

In simple words: giving form to the material.
Using visual elements
as the composer uses the scale.

For example:

a 4: interchange two of the 16 elements.
Namely 8 and 9. The sequence is broken.
The change of place of the two elements
determines the change of value of the entire series.

But order is maintained, and symmetry preserved
It has only become more complex,
let us say more differentiated.

a 5: The one-dimensional series
contains many possible constellations (factorial 16)
but few order principles.

One of these is Arp's Law of Chance.
Random rearrangement causes all the elements
to change their position
without detectable equilibrium.

a 6: The same: each element changes its position,
but not its order.
The sequence is preserved, but reversed:

a left-right problem
as meaningless geometrically as it is optically.
(But it may be significant psychologically.)

a 7: A cyclic permutation of the series.
I.e. the right taken away and added to the left:
in this case exactly half.

The ends meet; they provide maximum contrast.
The ends no longer form terminal limits;
they are joined by an imaginary path
from grey to grey via infinity.

a 8: A reciprocatory arrangement.
With white in the middle,
and the next darkest shade

placed alternately on the left and right:
giving a dark end on each side.
In figures: ....6–4–2–1–3–5–7....

a 9: The series with the elements interspersed.
I.e. with the lighter and
darker halves regularly interposed.

The intervals between successive shades are greater,
with four, then three (then four again and so on)
shade gradations between adjacent elements.

a 10: The next example is like a 9.
The darker half has been rotated through 180 degrees.
Thus two operations are used for a single grouping:
interposition and rotation.

The shade gradations are different;
once again regular, but following a different rule:
This arrangement contains
both the greatest and the smallest contrasts.

One step further removed
from the original arrangement:
(see above) increasing the scope for conscious design.

Instead of retaining the elements in their original
one-dimensional row,
they can be grouped in a two-dimensional field.
There is no longer a self-contained order.
But there are more possibilities:
the relationships between the elements are multiplied.

As well as a one-dimensional
left-to-right proximity we now have
the top-to-bottom and the diagonal proximities
giving two-dimensional interrelationships.
While in the line series each element has two neighbour
(and each end element only one),
on the field it will have
eight if it is in the centre,
five if it is on the edge,
and three if it is in the corner.

b 1: If it is folded upon itself like a jointed rod
the line series becomes a two-dimensional grouping
but with its one-dimensional origin still discernible.

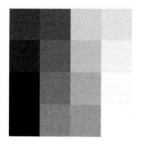

The jointed-rod principle can be generally defined
as a line coiled down
on a field of 4 x 4 units.
Following the rule
that the line must pass
through each of the 16 positions;

it may not be broken,
or intersect itself.

This principle can be utilised
to give a finite number of variations.
Some of them: b 2 to b 5.

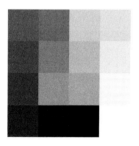

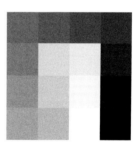

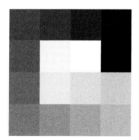

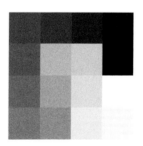

b 6: Special case of the jointed rod:
a right-angled spiral

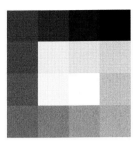

b 7: A double spiral

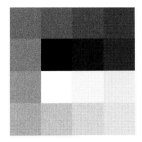

b 8: The jointed rod folded diagonally

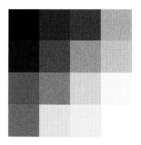

b 9: The line series has been divided into four
equal sections,
and the sections placed side by side.

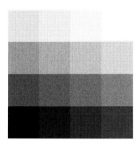

b 10: The arrangement takes on
a more characteristic appearance
once the order of the line series is abandoned.
The elements interspersed
in two dimensions

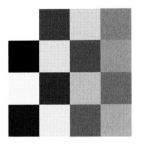

b 11: A "magic square".
(A puzzle familiar from the schoolroom:
each horizontal, vertical and diagonal
column of four elements always adds up to 34.
If the four shades in each column are "added together"
their sum is always the same shade of grey.)

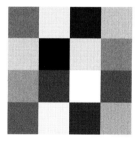

b 12: A random arrangement.
Here: a grouping obtained by shuffling numbers.

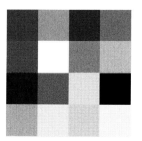

Sixteen different elements grouped in a field
and moved around;
the field defined
(in this case 4 x 4, though others would be possible):
the number of possible ways
of grouping the elements in a line series is finite.
The formula is constant: factorial 16,
which nevertheless gives
20 922 400 000 000 different possibilities.
Programming a problem
means planning in stages.
(With feedback, of course.)
The first stage is the material in its original form.
(With colours, for example, it is the colour solid.)
From stage to stage experience is accumulated,
and each stage provides material for the next.

Four like groups added together:
a group composed of groups.
Or: a structure composed of structures.

In the first place groups are formed from groups
by symmetrical replication.

The requirement remains the same:
to stay within the two dimensions of the surface.

The space dimension is not taken into account.
That means: even if it is not intentionally included
it is automatically incorporated;
its presence is virtual, not actual,
but perceived nevertheless:
it is not possible to visualise all the shades
as lying in the same plane.
But it is left to the beholder
to choose which shades are in the "foreground"
and which in the "background".

Group b 1 is

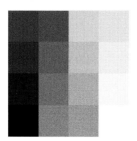

c 1: reflected

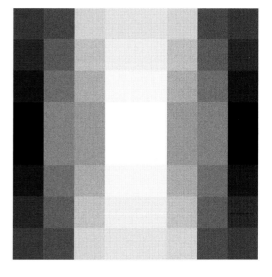

c 2: rotated

c 3: displaced.

Limiting the number of replications to four
is of little importance when the group is displaced.
When it is rotated or reflected
more and less complex units are thereby produced.
That means: by the addition of the individual groups
a whole is formed that is more than the sum of its parts.

In the second place groups are formed from groups
by integration on the larger field.
That means: in examples c 1 to c 3
the sixteen-element group b 1
is replicated as a whole four times
and by an operation of symmetry
the four groups are combined together
to form a new whole.
The new field measures 8 x 8 units.

Instead of being regarded as a result, this field
may be used as a starting point.
Instead of placing together
four groups of 16 elements
the groups may be broken up and
the 64 elements distributed
at will over the entire field.

c 4: following the law of chance.

c 5: in groups with the like elements ordered
and interposed.

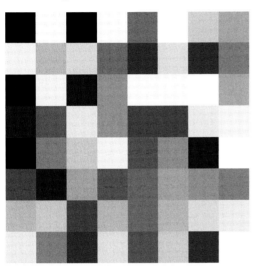

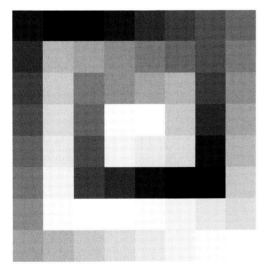

c 6: as alternately reversed series,
i.e. from white to black to white again in turn
and arranged as a spiral on the larger field.

c 7: grouped by an arbitrary act,
that is, following no definite rule
and yet not deliberately at random.
Composed, that is to say, as prompted "by feeling".

Examples c 1 to c 7
are not self-contained.
There is even less self-containedness
in the replicated groupings than in simple ones.
They demonstrate principles.
The possibilities are as uncountable
as their number is finite.
But here also general views can be obtained.

Following the practice of the surveyor,
the system of datums may be refined.
The lower orders of possible groupings
may be systematically placed between the higher orders

Each grouping
may be changed by a permutation
that may be more or less regular.

The reflected grouping c 1 is seen as a "negative" if

c 8: the order of the elements is reversed.

c 9: two vertical rows of c 1 have been taken
from the right and added to the left.

c 10: the basis is again c 1:
the black centre has been displaced
one element downwards.
All the other elements change their positions
following this first move.
The original symmetrical arrangement
has lost its horizontal axis;
the vertical axis is preserved.

It is also interesting
to examine the results of the same operation
carried out with other groups.
The line series of elements' arbitrarily coiled
in the sixteen-element groups
are reflected twice
and thus provided with an optimum degree of order,
i.e. the maximum degree
of symmetry relationships.

c 11: b 2 reflected

c 12: b 3 reflected

c 13: b 4 reflected

c 14: b 5 reflected

Example c 10 is a reflection with a single axis
of symmetry
obtained from c 1 by means of a permutation.
Single-axis symmetry of this kind
may also be obtained from first principles.

c 15: all the elements are divided into two halves;
they are coiled as desired in one half
and reflected in the other.

c 16: c 15 permutated

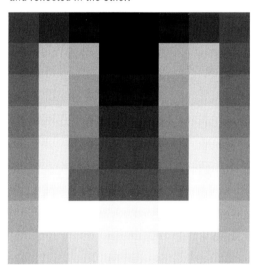

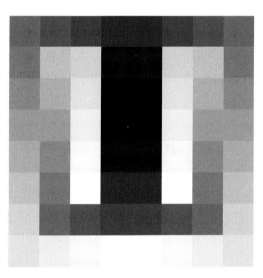

c 17: reflection along a diagonal.

c 18: reflected spirals.

Examples c 15 to c 18
are combinations of two different operations:
coiling and reflecting.

The following examples are of coiling,
or more precisely:
of spiralling combined with rotation,
with the spirals within one another
rather than adjacent to one another;
thus we have a third operation:
interpenetration.

c 19: two spirals mutually inverted at 180 degrees.

c 20: as c 19, with the sequence of the elements
in the second spiral reversed.

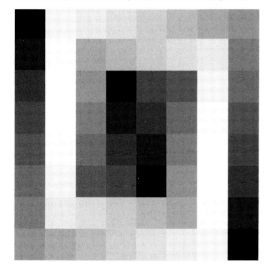

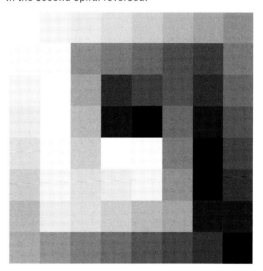

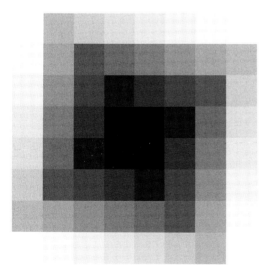

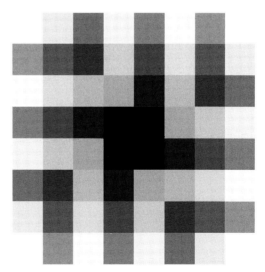

c 21: four spirals interpenetrating at 90 degrees.

c 22: as c 21, but using the line series a 10.
The figure has a transparent appearance.
The interpenetration of a 10
is potentiated.

A characteristic of groups of repeated elements: to the relationships between the different elements are added relationships between like elements.

These relationships may not only be taken as automatic results, but used as the basis of new groupings.

The total of 64 elements is composed of 16 groups of 4 like elements.
The operations consist in interposing them.

Because of their arrangement and the impression they give of spatial transparency (see c 22) let us call this type of grouping: interpenetration.

c 23: interpenetration and rotation in two halves.

c 24: interpenetration and rotation starting from a grey centre.

c 25: as c 24, in a permutated order, i.e. with a black-white centre as the starting point.

c 26: interpenetration of groups in graded zones.

Extension of the group
by repetition of the elements
is also possible.

In the examples the replication factor is 4.
Four is a special case
among x cases. See c 3.
But in decoration
bands of any length
or areas of unlimited size may be produced.

A second possibility
for extension within a bounded area:
to refine the original structure
instead of repeating the elements.
That is to say, to use more, i.e. smaller gradations,
between the extremes of black and white.

Interpenetration analogous to c 23
obtained with a basic structure of 28
instead of 16 elements.

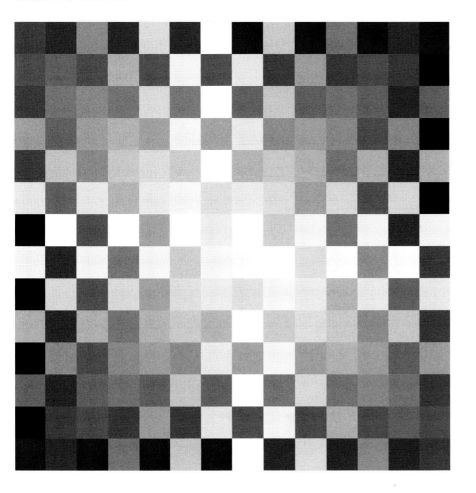

Each constellation is a combination
of free choice and predestined result;
of chance and order.

Each order is a special case
among all the possible groupings.
Determined by the combination of criteria,
as numerous and as self-contained as possible.
The more complex its principle,
the more typical is its configuration.
Its form.

Chance is a different matter.
It may be harnessed in any number of ways:
with dice, lots, a roulette wheel;
by using the telephone directory
or with the help of a blind person,
or the whims of a monkey –
the results will always be different,
but they will nonetheless be scarcely distinguishable.
We may perceive 1000 different kinds of order.
But the differences between ten chance arrangements
can be identified only with difficulty.

c 27: chessboard interpenetration.

c 28: the lighter half has been deprived of order,
and distributed according to chance.

c 29: as c 28, with the darker half
also in a chance distribution.
No element is any longer in its original position;
but the two halves are.
This is the criterion of order,
and its effect is preserved.

c 4: this final criterion has also been abandoned;
all the elements are mixed at random.

The interpenetration c 27
contains a particularly high degree of order.
This order is now reduced successively,
i.e. in the proportion in which
the chance component becomes more important.

These examples could be multiplied (almost) at will.
But just as the point of programming consists
in finding solutions to individual problems,
it is purposeless to show
all the individual solutions of a given programme.

The purpose is only
to reveal the innumerable variations
that can be obtained from a simple structure
by controlled movement.
To demonstrate the programme of a programme.
The advance from the material to the design.

Again:
The examples are based on a linear structure,
a series of 16 elements of equal size
and 16 equal gradations from white to black.
Without changing the elements,
the structure has been changed:
a in the line series itself,
b by substituting a two-dimensional order for the
   linear, and
c by repetition.

The elements may also be changed.
We may take x instead of 16,
or elements of different size instead of equal size,
or unequal gradations of shade
instead of equal gradations,
or a different colour series
instead of the black-white series.

All the possibilities can not (or hardly)
be considered at once, but only some of them.

Thus:
retain all the components,
but change only the colour series:
what are the possible variants?

The black-white series
is a special case, a part of a larger structure.
It occupies a precise position in the colour solid.
That is, in the complex order
of all perceivable colours.

The colour solid also contains
the following special cases:

– The one-dimensional closed series of
   the colour circle of pure colours.
– The open, one-dimensional series
   of the pure colours to black, or to white.
– The closed two-dimensional colour triangles
   from colours to black and white
   with all the resulting mixtures
   following the co-ordinates.

– The less individual structures
   that nevertheless exhibit a high degree of order:
   all kinds of related series, surfaces, elements.

For example:
half of a colour circle,
an open series from colour to complementary colour.
Or one-third, one-quarter of the colour circle.

Or:
There are many paths from a colour
to its complementary colour.
The most uniform follows
the circumference of the circle;
the shortest passes through grey.
But it need not follow either route.
Thus fixed points, say red, grey, green,
may be joined by sine curves.
In other words:
We may proceed from red to grey
not by the direct route
but via the red-yellow quadrant.
Each successive shade becomes not only greyer
but also yellower.
But the yellow converges with the grey.
On the other side the same movement
leads to green.
See page 91.

Or:
by following the same path,
but displacing the colours by one or more shades.
See pages 92 and 93.

Furthermore:
If designing is programming,
then the basis is the material.
That is, a precise knowledge of the material.
Colour, proportions, dimensions:
what are the other parameters?
What are the components?

Discovery is a part of design.
Let us mention one more:
texture,
i.e. the outward nature of the material,
its surface.

The same programme
that is based on the effects of colour
can be based on the effects of texture:
instead of different gradations of colour
differently derived light reflexes
following the same structure.
See pages 94 and 95.

And
so
on.

Thus the designer
proceeds from material to form?
And perhaps from form to art?
Where are the thresholds?

I do not know. (I do not want to know.)

If my pictures are not art:
that would be my misfortune.
(The price of my conviction.)

The c-structure of 64 elements
(I acknowledge it): I have declared it to be a picture.
I have christened it carro 64:

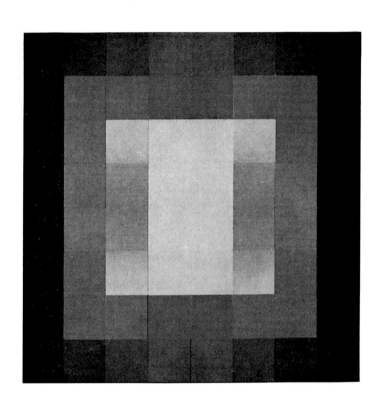

carro 64
black–white
1956-61

carro 64
red–grey–green
1956–61

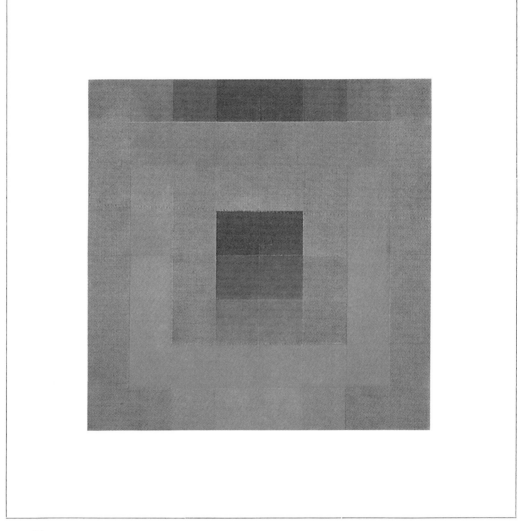

carro 64
red-grey-green
1956–61

carro 64
red-grey-blue
1962

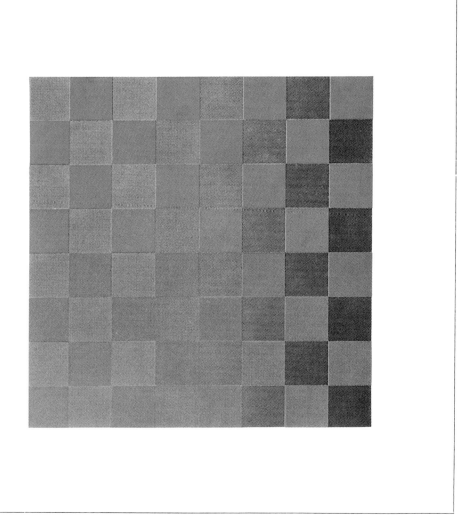

carro 64
red–grey–green
1956–61

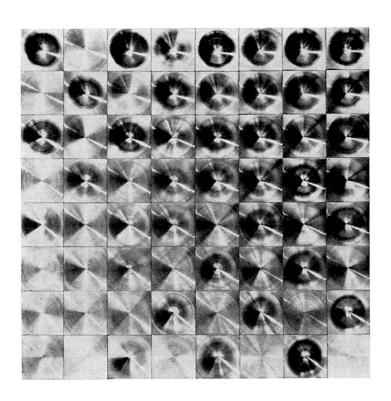

carro 64
turned metal
1962

(Inserat)

What does that mean:
I have declared carro 64 to be a picture?
What is a picture that has no binding form,
but consists of a countless number of constellations?
What does an original look like?

Like this:
64 loose precision-made cubes
each numbered 1–16 on the side,
are put together in a frame
and hung on the wall.

The beholder makes his own constellation.
Not every one is original,
because this one or that has already been found
by this or that beholder.

But carro 64 contains a reserve of original constellations;
more than several beholders will ever discover.
Thus what is original in carro 64 is the idea
and not the picture as a single item.
Thus in autumn 1962 120 copies were made
in the series yellow-grey-blue:
as a consequence of an art original in re-production
and at the same time as an experiment in a social art.
The beholder is not only to be included as a partner
but also to be in a position to buy the picture.

It costs DM 395.– until further notice.
There are at present (autumn 1963)
still 35 copies to be had from Christian Holzäpfel,
7273 Ebhausen, Bundesrepublik Deutschland
or from the Gallery Der Spiegel
Köln, Richartzstrasse 10
Western Germany.
Intending purchasers will be sent a prospectus.